REVELATION

JACK W. HAYFORD
Executive Editor

THOMAS NELSON
Since 1798

NASHVILLE   DALLAS   MEXICO CITY   RIO DE JANEIRO   BEIJING

Published in Nashville, Tennessee. Thomas Nelson is a trademark of Thomas Nelson, Inc.

Thomas Nelson, Inc. titles may be purchased in bulk for educational, business, fundraising, or sales promotional use. For information, please email SpecialMarkets@ThomasNelson.com.

Unless otherwise indicated, all Scripture quotations are from the New King James Version, copyright © 1979, 1980, 1982, 1990, 2004 by Thomas Nelson, Inc.

Hayford, Jack W.

Revelation

ISBN 13: 978-1-4185-3330-4

Printed in the United States of America
HB 01.24.2022

TABLE OF CONTENTS

PREFACE

When Will Jesus Return?

MATTHEW 25:13 exhorts and admonishes us to, "Watch therefore, for you know neither the day nor the hour in which the Son of Man is coming."

Throughout the centuries, people have interpreted "hour and day" to mean that we may discover a specific day, month or year when Jesus will return. Not so. We will not know for sure when Jesus will donne the skies with His Second Coming. Will be in our lifetime? Only the Father knows when Jesus will return.

However, Jesus began His sentence with the command, "Watch." The challenge the Lord gives us is to be constantly and eagerly waiting for His return. Therefore, our duty is twofold: to prepare ourselves for His coming, so that the Lord will receive a Bride without "spot or wrinkle" (Ephesians 5:27), and to "do business" until He returns, so that the kingdom of God is preserved and extended upon the earth (Luke 19:11–27). Let us be about the Father's business. Let us live in expectation of the Master's return. Let us be put away all idle speculation regarding the time of His coming, and instead prepare the way of the Lord.

We need only to focus on Jesus' promise in Revelation 22:20, "Surely I am coming quickly." This blessed hope, which was declared by angels and spoken of by the apostles, is tenderly reiterated by the Lord at the very end of His Word. It is as if He wished to say, "There is much in My Word that you need attend to, but do not let this hope be overshadowed: I am coming back soon." Together with John, let us say, "Even so, come, Lord Jesus!"

Keys of the Kingdom

KEYS CAN BE SYMBOLS of possession, of the right and ability to acquire, clarify, open or ignite. Keys can be concepts that unleash mind-boggling possibilities. Keys clear the way to a possibility otherwise obstructed!

Jesus spoke of keys: "And I will give you the keys of the kingdom of heaven, and whatever you bind on earth will be bound in heaven, and whatever you loose on earth will be loosed in heaven" (Matthew 16:19).

While Jesus did not define the "keys" He has given, it is clear that He did confer specific tools upon His church which grant us access to a realm of spiritual "partnership" with Him. The "keys" are concepts or biblical themes, traceable throughout Scripture, which are verifiably dynamic when applied with solid faith under the lordship of Jesus Christ. The "partnership" is the essential feature of this enabling grace; allowing believers to receive Christ's promise of "kingdom keys," and to be assured of the Holy Spirit's readiness to actuate their power in the life of the believer.

Faithful students of the Word of God, and some of today's most respected Christian leaders, have noted some of the primary themes which undergird this spiritual partnership. A concise presentation of many of these primary themes can be found in the Kingdom Dynamics feature of the *New Spirit-Filled Life Bible*. The *New Spirit-Filled Life Study Guide Series*, an outgrowth of this Kingdom Dynamics feature, provides a treasury of more in-depth insights on these central truths. This study series offers challenges and insights designed to enable you to more readily understand and appropriate certain dynamic "Kingdom Keys."

Each study guide has twelve to fourteen lessons, and a number of helpful features have been developed to assist you in your study, each marked by a symbol and heading for easy identification.

 Kingdom Key

KINGDOM KEY identifies the foundational Scripture passage for each study session and highlights a basic concept or principle presented in the text along with cross-referenced passages.

Kingdom Life

The KINGDOM LIFE feature is designed to give practical under-standing and insight. This feature will assist you in comprehending the truths contained in Scripture and applying them to your day-to-day needs, hurts, relationships, concerns, or circumstances.

 Word Wealth

The WORD WEALTH feature provides important definitions of key terms.

 Behind the Scenes

BEHIND THE SCENES supplies information about cultural beliefs and practices, doctrinal disputes, and various types of background information that will illuminate Bible passages and teachings.

 Kingdom Extra

The optional KINGDOM EXTRA feature will guide you to Bible dictionaries, Bible encyclopedias, and other resources that will enable you to gain further insight into a given topic.

 Probing the Depths

Finally, PROBING THE DEPTHS will present any controversial issues raised by particular lessons and cite Bible passages and other sources which will assist you in arriving at your own conclusions.

The New Spirit-Filled Life Study Guide is a comprehensive resource presenting study and life-application questions and exercises with spaces provided in the study guide to record your answers. These study guides are designed to provide all you need to gain a good, basic understanding of the covered theme and apply biblical counsel to your life. You will need only a heart and mind open to the Holy Spirit, a prayerful attitude, a pencil and a Bible to complete the studies and apply the truths they contain. However, you may want to have a notebook handy if you plan to expand your study to include the optional KINGDOM EXTRA feature.

The Bible study method used in this series employs four basic steps:

1. *Observation*. What does the text say?
2. *Interpretation*. What is the original meaning of the text?
3. *Correlation*. What light can be shed on this text by other Scripture passages?
4. *Application*. How should my life change in response to the Holy Spirit's teaching of this text?

The New King James Version is the translation used wherever Scripture portions are cited in the *New Spirit-Filled Life Kingdom Dynamics Study Guide* series. Using this translation with this series will make your study easier, but it is certainly not imperative and you will profit through use of any translation you choose.

Through Bible study, you will grow in your essential understanding of the Lord, His kingdom and your place in it; but you need more. Jesus was sent to teach us "all things" (John 14:26; 1 Corinthians 2:13). Rely on the Holy Spirit to guide your study and your application of the Bible's truths. Bathe your study time in prayer as you use this series to learn of Him and His plan for your life. Ask the Spirit of God to illuminate the text, enlighten your mind, humble your will, and comfort your heart. And as you explore the Word of God and find the keys to unlock its riches, may the Holy Spirit fill every fiber of your being with the joy and power God longs to give all His children. Read diligently on. Stay open and submissive to Him. Learn to live your life as the Creator intended. You will not be disappointed. He promises you!

ADDITIONAL OBSERVATIONS

INTRODUCTION

Understand the Prophetic

THE LESSONS WHICH FOLLOW will guide you on a study of the great future events in store for the Jews, the Gentiles, and the church as revealed in the great prophetic books of Daniel and Revelation and realized in the exciting events of current history. You will find these studies of mankind's future to be balanced and believable. Each one is focused on a careful exposition of Scripture and not merely the rehearsal of a human system of interpretation.

We want to gain a whole new appreciation for prophetic truth, while allowing it to do what it is ultimately designed for—to change the way we live "until the end of time."

Guidelines

It is natural and fitting to study Daniel and Revelation together since something from every chapter in Daniel is either quoted or shares striking similarities to Revelation.

Daniel interpreted dreams and *Revelation* is the account of a vision (or series of visions) given by God to John. Each of these spiritual experiences is communicated with strange symbols and figures of speech. Though biblical prophecy has been supernaturally revealed, inspired, and illuminated in our hearts by the Light of the World and by His Spirit of Truth, some passages are admittedly hard to understand. We need some guidelines for interpreting prophecy.

1. The most important guideline for studying prophecy is to **seek the plain and normal meaning of the words and situations described within their historical context.** Don't come to a prophetic passage with a preconceived conclusion or interpretive system to force it into. Let the grammatical and historical

context communicate the plain and normal meaning, and then incorporate that meaning into what you already know.

2. **Compare one prophecy with another, especially similar prophecies.** Each prophecy unfolds a bit more of the total plan of God for the ages. Often there are overlapping and corresponding references in a few or several prophecies, though they may have been delivered hundreds of years apart. (Compare the description of "the Ancient of Days" in Daniel 7:9–14 with the "One like the Son of Man" in Revelation 1:13–16 and the Lamb in chapter 5:8–14.)

3. **Remember that the timing of the fulfillment may be uncertain.** From God's side of eternity the elements are complete and the prophecy is already fact. From man's side, separate future events may seem to blend into one, as a person looking toward a range of mountains may see two peaks as one, not perceiving the valley between them or its size and characteristics. This principle suggests that biblical prophecies may have several layers of fulfillment. (Examples of this difference in time perception may be found in Isaiah 9:6–9; 11:1–5; 61:1–3 and Luke 4:16–21.)

4. The final guideline is sometimes called **the law of double reference.** A prophecy may have fulfillment both in the time of the prophet, and another in the perhaps distant future. For instance, the prophetic sign given to Ahaz in Isaiah 7:14 also refers both to the birth of a son by Isaiah's wife (Isaiah 8:3), and to the birth of the Messiah by the Virgin Mary (Matthew 1:22; Luke 1:27). Examples of this can also be found in Deuteronomy 28:58, 64–66 and 1 John 2:18.

 Probing the Depths

Many devoted Christians are surprised to discover that other equally dedicated believers view the prophetic words of Scripture differently. The prophetic words of Scripture tolerate a wide spectrum of approaches, but the common denominator of all is the ultimate triumph of Jesus Christ, who culminates history with His final coming and reigns with and through His church forever.

The most popularized and widely discussed approach to interpreting biblical, end-time prophecy is called the *Dispensationalist* interpretation. This proposes that the church will be translated to heaven when Jesus returns "in the air" (1 Thessalonians 4:17). This event is often referred to as the "Rapture." Chapters 6—8 of Revelation are perceived by Dispensationalists as descriptive of the Great Tribulation (Matthew 24:21) or the wrath of God (1 Thessalonians 5:9) from which believers will be protected (Revelation 3:10). This approach sees national Israel as God's people on Earth at this time (since the Church of Jesus Christ will have been raptured). This interpretive approach understands that national Israel will be restored to Jerusalem and protected by the divine seal (Revelation 7:1–8), will worship in a rebuilt temple (Revelation 11:1–3), and will suffer at the hand of the Antichrist.

Not as widely published, but at least equally widely believed is the *Moderate Futurist* view. This proposes that the Book of Revelation summarizes the conclusion of the Church's age-long procession through tribulation and triumph, warfare, and victory, and culminating in the climactic return of Jesus Christ for His church. The tribulation is generally viewed as age-long, but increasing in intensity, so that the church is understood as present through much of Earth's turmoil until just prior to the outpouring of the "bowls full of the wrath of God" (Revelation 15:7). This culminates in the collapse of the present world order (Revelation chapters 16—18).

Among other views are these:

1. The *Historic* position sees biblical prophecy as a symbolic prophecy of the whole of church history, including all the events and movements that have shaped the conflict and progress of the Christian Church.
2. The *Preterist* views biblical prophecy as a message of hope and comfort to first-century believers only, offering them an expectation of their deliverance from Roman persecution and oppression.
3. The *Idealist* formulates no particular historical focus or effort at interpreting specifics of prophecy, rather seeing it as a broad, poetic portrayal of the conflict between the kingdom of God and the powers of satan.

The Times of the Gentiles

"The times of the Gentiles," as presented in Daniel, is the biblical designation for a period of time between the destruction of Jerusalem in A.D. 70 (some identify it with the beginning with the Babylonian Captivity in 606 B.C.) and the Second Coming of Christ. This interval is defined by the Lord Jesus Christ as the time when Jerusalem (the city of peace) would be controlled by Gentile world powers (Luke 21:24). Many see the return of the Old City of Jerusalem to Jewish control in June of 1967 as being the end of "the times of the Gentiles" and are awaiting the imminent return of Christ.

Daniel is instructed by God to "shut up the words, and seal the book, until the time of the end" (Daniel 12:4). Many feel this means that much of the detail in the book of Daniel will be obscure and irrelevant until the events of the final stage of Gentile world power remove the seal and the book of Daniel becomes fully intelligible.

Prepare for the Journey

In preparation for the incredible journey of discovery as we travel the road of biblical prophecy, read the book of Daniel and the Book of Revelation.

Daniel

Keep in mind that chapters 2 through 7 of Daniel are the report of the development of Daniel's character and prophetic skills. Chapters 8 through 12 contain his series of visions about future kingdoms and events. In these final chapters, Daniel emerges as a key prophetic book for understanding much of the Bible. Many insights into end-times prophecies are dependent upon an understanding of this book.

Revelation

The Book of Revelation is a series of vivid visions given to the apostle John. It is a cosmic pageant—an elaborate, colorful series of tableaux, accompanied and interpreted by celestial speakers and singers. All the visions of John contain figurative language, signs and symbols pointing to spiritual realities. This way of communicating is essential because spiritual truth and unseen reality must always be communicated to human beings through their senses—we cannot mentally grasp those things that are completely alien to our knowledge and experience.

Both these books point to the sovereignty of God and His ultimate control over all peoples and nations. Both bring hope and comfort to the children of God for both look forward to the day when our salvation is complete and our Lord gathers us to Himself to rule and reign with Him throughout eternity.

ADDITIONAL OBSERVATIONS

The Source

Kingdom Key—*Prophecy Is the Revelation of God*

2 Peter 1:20, 21 Knowing this first, that no prophecy of Scripture is of any private interpretation, for prophecy never came by the will of man, but holy men of God spoke as they were moved by the Holy Spirit.

Mankind seems to have an insatiable interest in future and unusual events. Consequently, many are deliberately or demonically deceived by charlatans who prey on these unsuspecting souls. These false prophets dish out heresy, truth laced with error.

Biblical prophecy is vastly different. Its predictions are not only reliable, but divinely inspired. Biblical prophecy will always meet four conditions:

1. It will be spoken before the event takes place
2. It will contain concrete details to exclude guesswork
3. There will be sufficient time between prediction and fulfillment to affirm the facts
4. It will be an unveiling of the future which excludes mere rational human foresight

Word Wealth—*Prophecy*

Prophecy: Hebrew *nebuwah* (neb-oo-ah); Strong's #5016: a spoken or written prediction; may also be used for an inspired teaching. *Nebuwah* has at its root the Hebrew word *naba* meaning to speak by inspiration. True prophecy is a direct, unobstructed, unfiltered message from God to an individual. Prophecy may come through dreams or visions, revelational insight, ecstatic experiences, as well as through creative, artistic modes. Rarely in modern times is the voice of God heard audibly, although this manner of receiving prophecy is chronicled throughout Scripture.

Prophecy: Greek *Propheteia* (prof-ay-ti'-ah); Strong's #4394: The strict meaning of this word is "prediction." However, prophecy is not only foretelling, it is the declaration of that which cannot be known by natural, cognitive or intellectual means. *Propheteia* is more the "forth-telling" of the will of God, whether with reference to the past, present, or future.

Kingdom Life—*Earnestly Desire Prophecy*

Some people object to the study of prophecy. Many believe the prophetic gift is fulfilled with the revelation of Jesus Christ, and through the canonization of the Scriptures. They say it is unprofitable, leading men and women to become dreamers and charlatans. They claim focusing on prophecy distorts reality and diverts sincere believers from service and activity in the work of the church today.

There always have been students of Scripture who became so obsessed with prophecies of the future that they have neglected the present purposes of God. Their quest for spiritual understanding becomes inordinately focused on solely pursuing matters of the eschaton or future, end times events of the kingdom of God. The key is always balance, discernment, and wisdom when approaching the study and understanding of Holy Scriptures.

Still others scoff at prophecy. They see it as mere writings of man, hard to comprehend with certainty. Yet, God seems to consider prophecy to be important. More than one quarter of the canon of Scripture was prophetic prediction when it was written. In both the Old and New Testaments there are whole books which are, in essence, prophecies (for example, Zechariah, 1 Thessalonians, Revelation). Some have estimated that nearly ninety percent of the events prophesied in the Bible have not yet been fulfilled.

Behind the Scenes

Although certain books are recognized as being predominately prophetic in content, prophecy is found throughout the Bible. It has been calculated that Scripture contains about 165,000 words of predictive prophecy. This number is nearly equivalent to two thirds of the entire text of the New Testament. Few realize that the books of Matthew, Mark, and Luke contain more prophetic material than the entire Book of Revelation.

Using a trusted concordance, locate passages in these three Gospels that are prophetic. Make note of what is revealed so that you may refer to your insights as you progress through this study.

Kingdom Life—*Prophecy Directs Toward Christ*

In Revelation 19:10 we learn that "the testimony of Jesus is the spirit of prophecy." In a very real way, these words in Revelation define Scripture. Jesus Christ is at the center of all: past, present and future. He is at the center of both the Old and New Testament as the the purpose of both is to reveal Him to the world. Therefore, all utterances claiming to be true prophecy will point to the Christ. He is the Alpha and Omega, the Beginning and End of all things. Jesus is synonymous with, or at the heart of, anything truly prophetic.

Read 1 John 4:1–6; Hebrews 13:8; Revelation 19:10.

Questions:

What will be the overriding message of any true prophecy?

_____

_____

_____

_____

_____

From God's perspective, what is the intended result of predictive prophecy?

_____

_____

_____

_____

_____

Record Your Thoughts

There are many "prophetic" voices today predicting future events. We must guard our minds and spirits from influences that do not find their source in our Heavenly Father. Jesus warned that there would be many false prophets in the last days claiming His authority and insight. We must learn to recognize the Voice of Truth from deceptive words.

Locate all that Jesus said regarding false teachers and prophets in the last days. Make note of the tools we are to use to guard our hearts and minds from their destructive influence.

SESSION TWO

The Purpose

 Kingdom Key—*Possess the Promise*

2 Timothy 4:8 Finally, there is laid up for me the crown of righteousness, which the Lord, the righteous Judge, will give to me on that Day, and not to me only but also to all who have loved His appearing.

Eschatology is that aspect of biblical doctrine dealing with "last things" (from Greek *eschatos*, "final"). Vital Christians in every generation have lived in immediate anticipation of Christ's Second Coming. Each era since Christ's ascension has seen evidence which seemed to argue that any could be the concluding generation. This is not an unhealthy attitude: Christ Jesus desires that people expectantly anticipate His return. It is this anticipation which will prompt us in a powerful way to live our lives in such a way that we are ready, at any moment, to meet Christ Jesus, our Savior and Lord.

Read Matthew 25:1–13; 2 Peter 3:10–18.

Questions:

When you consider the immanent return of Christ, what thoughts and feelings do you experience?

✎ _____

_____

_____

_____

_____

_____

What do these thoughts and feeling reveal about your relationship to the Lord?

✎_____

_____

_____

_____

_____

In what way do these thoughts and feelings impact your daily walk with the Lord?

✎_____

_____

_____

_____

_____

An Unknown Time

Christians of all ages, like Paul ("we who are alive," 1 Thessalonians 4:15), have confidently awaited the return of Christ in their own time. Throughout the history of the church, there have been those who deprived the return of Christ of its intended force by setting dates or specifying limits. Those of any age who do so are claiming to know more than Jesus Himself: "But of that day and hour no one knows, not even the angels in heaven, nor the Son, but only the Father" (Mark 13:32).

However, two things are certain: 1) the return of Christ is an assured future event, and 2) that event is closer than it has ever been before.

The Decisive Event

Eschatology shows how God's Redeemer will establish His kingdom upon a rebellious earth. The long process through which God selected a righteous group to serve Him on earth came to a climax in the person of Christ. He is indeed "God with us" (Matthew 1:23). This phrase from Isaiah 7:14 spoke of God's presence in Jesus in order to save (Isaiah 9:6–7) and to judge (Isaiah 7:17; 8:6–8).

Christ's first coming was to save (Mark 10:45); His second will be primarily to rule. But His return will also spell relief to His faithful remnant. Eschatology shows that God's presence for the redeemed will be fully realized at Jesus' return, when He will dwell among all the redeemed in the new heavens and earth (Revelation 21:3).

Above all, the victory of Christ's Cross is the decisive eschatological event. In it the curse was reversed, and ever since, God has been progressively accomplishing His judgment against the forces of wickedness in heaven and earth.

Record Your Thoughts

The point of eschatology throughout the Bible is to provide encouragement to believers in their witness for Jesus Christ (Matthew 24:14; 1 Corinthians 15:58). It is not mentioned to encourage idle speculation or controversy. The reason God grants us a view of the future is to encourage us to witness for Christ and serve Him in the present.

Questions:

What has been your reaction to reading biblical prophecy in the past?

✎ _____

_____

_____

_____

How can focusing more on the event than the promises cause us to miss God's intended message?

✎ _____

_____

_____

_____

_____

ADDITIONAL OBSERVATIONS

The Focus

Kingdom Key—*Prepare Your Heart*

Ephesians 5:25–26 ". . . Christ also loved the church and gave Himself for her, that He might sanctify and cleanse her with the washing of water by the word, that He might present her to Himself, a glorious church . . ."

God's Word has been unscrolled in both the Scriptures and in His incarnate Son—Jesus Christ. Jesus described the importance of the eternal Scriptures and He also commended the steadfast inquiry into the Word of God. There is no such thing as health or growth in Christian living apart from a clear priority on the place of the Bible in the life of the individual or the group. The Scriptures are the conclusive standard for our faith, morals, and practical living and are the nourishment for our rising to strength in faith, holiness in living, and effectiveness in service.

Read Matthew 4:4; John 5:39; Psalm 119:15–16.

Questions:

Describe how you can be washed "by the water of the word."

_____

_____

_____

What are the benefits of reading and knowing God's word?

_____

_____

_____

Meet Daniel

Read Daniel 1.

The Book of Daniel begins with a description of a sorrowful situation. The people of Judah had turned from the Lord and had become a wicked and unrighteous nation. As a result God allowed Nebuchadnezzar, the King of pagan Babylon, to set siege to and finally defeat Jerusalem. Thousands died of famine and disease during the siege and many more were killed when Nebuchadnezzar overtook Jerusalem.

Following Nebuchadnezzar's victory many of the people were taken captive into Babylon. History indicates that fifty to seventy of the finest young men from Jewish royalty and nobility were chosen to be trained for three years in preparation for royal service. They were to be fed from the king's own choice food and wine (food likely dedicated to the worship of false gods). They were kept healthy and were well cared for. However, these young men were most likely castrated as was the custom for captives chosen to serve in the court of the king.

Among those chosen for service to Nebuchadnezzar were: Daniel, Hananiah, Mishael and Azariah. The meanings of these four names contain reference to God and express praise to Yahweh. Their names were changed to reflect praise to the false gods of Babylon. These committed servants of the one true God, were indoctrinated into the pagan culture of Babylon. Every effort was made to strip away their manhood, identity and even their faith.

 Kingdom Life—*Stand on the Word*

Daniel had learned God's law at an early age; reciting its words and memorizing its truths As a result, he had developed a very strong foundation of faith and lived his life in obedience to the Word of God. He remained unceasingly faithful and made no exception when his captors demanded that he break God's law and eat forbidden foods. Rather than defile himself, Daniel sought another way. He did not walk in defiance or disobedience but, choosing the attitude of a servant, he requested permission from his captor to abstain from the food provided by Nebuchadnezzar.

Daniel risked all to stand firm in his faith. He did not fear man, but chose to obey the law of God. Daniel's religious roots and spiritual heritage helped him resolve in his heart not to compromise and defile himself with even royal "delicacies." As far as we know, only Daniel, Shadrach, Meshach, and Abed-Nego took a stand to separate themselves toward the Lord and away from the things which would defile them. The rest of the hostages became "good Chaldeans" and went into obscurity. But by standing on the Word of God, the integrity, character, and faith of these three teenagers are read about and studied to this day!

Read 1 Thessalonians 4:1–12; Colossians 3:1–1.

Questions:

What things of the world are difficult for you to refuse, even though you know them to be harmful or disobedient?

_____

_____

_____

_____

What can you learn from Daniel and his friends that will enable you to stand strong before temptation?

_____

_____

_____

_____

Kingdom Extra—*Read It! Study It! Memorize It!*

The Bible—God's inspired Word—is the only conclusive source of wisdom, knowledge, and understanding concerning ultimate realities. It is a fountainhead of freeing truth and a gold mine of practical principles, waiting to liberate and/or enrich the person who will pursue its truth and wealth. The only way to healthy, balanced living is through the "rightly dividing" (Greek *orthotomounta,* literally, "cutting straight") of God's Word. Such correct, straight-on application of God's Word is the result of diligent study. We are called beyond casual approaches to the Scriptures, and should refuse to suit the Bible to our own convenience or ideology.

Paul told Timothy to "Give attention to reading (God's Word)," but he went much further and emphasized the importance of studying like a "worker" (from Greek *ergon* meaning "toil, effort"). Paul encourages all of us to give concerted time and energy to the task of learning and internalizing the Word of God.

Memorizing the Word of God is a mighty deterrent against sin. Memorizing Scripture also provides an immediate availability of God's "words" as a sword, ready in witnessing and effective in spiritual warfare.

Read 2 Timothy 2:15; John 8:32; Psalms 19:10; 119:11; Hebrews 4:12; Ephesians 6:17.

Questions:

How well do you know Scripture?

✎ _____

_____

_____

Is it ingrained in you to the point where it is a ready weapon in times of warfare?

✎ _____

_____

_____

_____

What steps can you take to become more familiar with the Word of God?

✎ _____

_____

_____

_____

_____

_____

Probing the Depths—*The Word of God*

All Scripture is *theopneustos* (Greek), which literally means "God-breathed." Each writer involved in the production of the Holy Scriptures was "moved by" (literally, "being borne along") the Holy Spirit. This does not mean that the writers were merely robots, seized upon by God's power to write automatically without their conscious participation. God does not override the gifts of intellect and sensitivity that He has given His creatures. (Beware of all instances where individuals claim to "automatically" write anything at any time, for the Holy Spirit never functions that way.) The very words used in the giving of the Bible (not just the ideas, but the precise terminology) were planned by the Holy Spirit, who deployed the respective authors to write the books of the Bible.

The Bible is: 1) Inerrant (perfect), which means that, in the original copies of each manuscript written by each Bible book's respective author, there was nothing mistaken or tinged with error. (Further, through the Holy Spirit's protection, the copies of Scripture delivered into our hands today remain essentially unchanged from archaic manuscripts. Even literary critics who claim no faith in the truth of the Bible, attest to its being the most completely reliable of any book transmitted from antiquity, in terms of its actually remaining unchanged and dependably accurate.) 2) Infallible, which refers to the fact that the Bible is unfailing as an absolutely trustworthy guide for our faith (belief in God) and practice (life and behavior).

Read 2 Timothy 3:16; 2 Peter 1:20–21; 1 Corinthians 2:10–13.

Questions:

What problems exist when one does not accept Scripture as the inerrant and infallible Word of God?

What are the benefits of believing these truths?

✎ _____

_____

_____

_____

_____

_____

Record Your Thoughts

Reading Scripture is of utmost importance to the Christian who desires a closer, more effective walk. If you have not already done so, make a commitment now to read at least 15 minutes a day for the next 30 days. At the end of that time, note the difference in your outlook and your walk.

Questions:

✎ _____

_____

_____

_____

_____

_____

_____

The Message
Daniel 1:1—6:28

Kingdom Key—*Seek and Surrender*

Luke 11:2 "Your Kingdom come, Your will be done."

The words of Jesus in this prayer are more than a suggestion to pray for a distant millennial day. This powerful statement transcends time. These are words of trust and surrender, for today and all tomorrows.

C. S. Lewis said, "There are only two kinds of people: those who say to God, 'Thy will be done,' and those to whom God ultimately says, '*Thy* will be done.'" How startling it is to weigh the implications of our *seeking* and *surrendering* to the rule of God in our hearts. To *invite* His kingly reign is to receive its forgiving, freeing and ennobling purposes for our lives. To *ignore* Him assures our self-rule, and thereby it's pitiful, painful, and destructive results.

Kingdom praying begins to find its power when we have come to the place of clear priority: "*Your* kingdom come!" It's often difficult to come to God's throne without our own "wish list"—our personal agendas of how we think things ought to be. But true kingdom praying comes to its highest possibility when we bow our lowest in surrender.

Daniel Hears from God

Daniel's relationship with God was such that he remained in communication with His Heavenly Father. Daniel sought God's will and obeyed His promptings. As a result, Daniel's "spiritual eyes and ears" were opened to the things of God.

Dreams had a prominent place in the lives of ancient peoples. They were considered to convey messages from God, and were frequently thought to be predictive in nature. Because of that, the images, thoughts, and impressions conveyed during dreams were often interpreted and pondered—especially when experienced by religious and political leaders.

Among the ancient Babylonians, Daniel became known as an interpreter of dreams. He and the other Hebrew "children" were known to be among the wisest of the king's advisors, but Daniel's gift of "understanding in all visions and dreams" (Daniel 1:17, 20) made him especially important during the reigns of Nebuchadnezzar, and the kings who followed him during Daniel's lifetime.

Questions:

Have you ever heard a message from the Lord in a dream or vision?

_____

_____

_____

How did that message impact your life?

_____

_____

_____

_____

_____

_____

Kingdom Life—*Be Ready*

Read Daniel 2:17–49.

When put to the test, Daniel was prayed-up, equipped and ready to meet the demand of Nebuchadnezzar. He knew the Lord could be trusted and would answer his prayer. He knew from experience!

Read John 14:13; Hebrews 1:6; Matthew 21:21–22.

Questions:

What is the biblical definition of "believe?" (Use a Bible dictionary or Strong's Concordance to find the answer.)

✎_____

_____

_____

In what ways is your prayer life lacking?

✎_____

_____

_____

_____

 Probing the Depths—*Nebuchadnezzar's Dream*

Nebuchadnezzar's dream contains the most comprehensive revelation of Gentile world history found anywhere in the Bible. It is a prophetic panorama which stretches from more than 600 years before Christ's first coming, to His millennial reign after His Second Coming. This "dream of destiny" affirms that God is in control of world affairs, and human history is really "His story."

Many dispensational scholars readily recognize the implied empires Nebuchadnezzar saw as a comprehensive history of four successive world empires spanning centuries: Babylon (gold head), Persia (silver chest and arms), Greece (bronze belly and thighs), Rome (iron legs), followed by the feet of iron and clay—an apt description of today's unstable global community. All that remains is for the Stone from heaven to strike the feet—collapsing the entire statue—and to become a Mountain that fills the Earth (the Second Coming). As the prophesied earthly powers come and go, in contrast, the kingdom of Christ will come and remain forever! As Nebuchadnezzar said, "Truly your God is the God of gods, the Lord of kings, and the revealer of secrets [mysteries]!"

Read Daniel 2:44; 7:27; 1 Corinthians 15:24; Revelation 11:15.

Question:

What do these verses indicate that God wants us to comprehend most about His kingdom?

✎ _____

_____

_____

Kingdom Life—*Resist the Enemy*

Read Daniel 3.

God's providence had established Nebuchadnezzar as the leading ruler of his time, but Nebuchadnezzar's power and position caused him to become filled with pride. Obsessed with his own glory, he determined to exalt himself in the eyes of the people by building a skyscraper-size, golden statue—a symbol of his power and the perpetuity of his kingdom.

The absolute refusal of Daniel's three friends to bow to the image, offers an inspiring illustration for believers. Satan, as the god of this age, forms many images by which he seeks to intimidate us and seduce us into bowing to the spirit of the world. Jesus Christ stands as the consummate example of the uncompromising commitment to resisting this tactic of the adversary. Jesus relied on prayer and the power of the Word of God to resist the temptation of the enemy. It is a close, prayerful relationship with the Lord that enables us to withstand and defeat Satan.

Read 2 Corinthians 4:3–4; 1 Corinthians 10:12–14; Luke 10:19; James 4:7.

Questions:

What things of the world most entice you?

✎ _____

_____

_____

_____

What commitments can you make that will enable you to stand firm and resist the tactics of satan?

_____

_____

_____

_____

Kingdom Extra

When Shadrach, Meshach, and Abed-Nego were thrown into the "fiery furnace," a fourth man was seen by Nebuchadnezzar. This is a dramatic illustration of the personal presence and protection of the Lord with His people who suffer for their testimony. The fourth man is a "Christophany" or a pre-incarnate appearance of the Messiah. Even Nebuchadnezzar recognized Him to be "like the Son of God." His later designation that this man was an "Angel" does not negate the possibility of this man being the pre-incarnate Christ.

Nebuchadnezzar's Second Dream

Read Daniel 4.

Although Nebuchadnezzar had seen the miraculous works of Yahweh and believed that it was the Spirit of the Holy God who gave Daniel his ability to interpret dreams, his own heart was still filled with pride. He had not submitted the rulership over his own kingdom to the kingdom of God. God dealt with him about his pride and exalted opinion of his rulership in the vision of a great tree, which symbolized both him and his dynasty.

Daniel's interpretation of this dream shows God's merciful attitude even toward arrogant pagans, as well as His desire that world powers surrender control to His lordship.

Nebuchadnezzar's pride reasserted itself and, even as he boasted in his mighty power, the judgment prophesied by Daniel fell upon him. He became insane, began to behave like an animal, and was banished from the very society over which he had exercised rulership.

Read Proverbs 8:13; 16:17–19; 1 John 2:15–17.

Questions:

In what ways do you find yourself falling victim to pride?

_____

_____

_____

_____

How does this affect your relationship with the Lord?

_____

_____

_____

How can you combat this tendency in your life?

_____

_____

_____

_____

Kingdom Life—*Offer True Prayer to God*

Often, prayer is seen as more of a wish list we present to God than a communion of heart. True prayer is the vehicle through which our hearts come into agreement and surrender to the heart of God. At the very root of prayer should be our desire that the will of God be done.

When Nebuchadnezzar's seven years of insanity ended, he declared that God "does according to His will." Nebuchadnezzar recognized God's dominion and right to rule and praised His majesty. It is not clear from Nebuchadnezzar's words whether he had a personal, on-going relationship with the Lord. However, it is clear that his restoration is designed to show God's ideal for all—surrender of our pride and desires into the hands of God. May His will be done on earth as it is in heaven.

Read Matthew 6:9–3.

Questions:

What do you learn from Jesus' example of true prayer?

_____

_____

_____

What is the heart attitude of Jesus' prayer?

_____

_____

_____

Where is the focus of this prayer?

_____

_____

_____

Blasphemy in Babylon

Read Daniel 5.

Belshazzar, whose name means "Bel Protect the King," reigned in Babylon during his father's 10-year absence from the throne. His irreverent use of the holy vessels stolen from the temple in Jerusalem brought forth a warning from the hand of God in the form of a disembodied hand and an unintelligible message. And great fear fell into the heart of Belshazzar.

His fear was well founded, for whatever God has sanctified is not to be profaned. What is set aside for the Lord's work should never be defiled by lesser use. Regarding holy things as common exhibits the same spirit which attributes the work of the Holy Spirit to satan. This is blasphemy because the Spirit's work is holy.

God Is Our Deliverer

Read Daniel 6.

Daniel was around eighty years old when Babylon was overtaken by Persia. Nebuchadnezzar's dream had come to pass—Babylon, the head of gold, was defeated. The Persian king, Darius, ruled the fallen empire.

Prompted by his government officials, king Darius decreed that no one in his kingdom should pray to any "god" but Darius himself for a period of thirty days. Anyone found not complying with this edict would be thrown into a den of lions. Daniel would not comply with this idolatrous decree and, three times that very day, knelt before God and prayed. King Darius, obliged to fulfill his oath, had the elderly prophet cast into the den of lions and sealed the entrance with a stone. But God delivered Daniel and as a result, King Darius decreed that throughout Persia the living God of Daniel would be recognized and feared.

Read Psalm 18:1–6.

Questions:

What "lions" exist in your own life that threaten to attack your faith and witness?

✎ _____

_____

_____

_____

_____

According to this Psalm, how can you find victory?

✎ _____

_____

_____

_____

Record Your Thoughts

Beginning now, and throughout the remainder of this study, make note in a journal of the areas in your life with which you struggle. One-by-one, search out the Scripture basis upon which you can find victory, seek the Lord in prayer and give the struggle against them over to the Lord. As you begin to realize victory in these areas, record the progress. By the end of this study, you may find long-standing battles have ceased to exist.

The Significance

Daniel 7—8:27

Kingdom Key—*Seek Understanding*

Proverbs 16:22 "Understanding is a wellspring of life to him who has it."

The word translated "wellspring" here can also be translated as "fountain." It denotes a naturally flowing channel. It brings to mind a crystal-clear stream flowing forth from out of the earth—a natural spring of life-giving water. Just as water results in productive and fruitful soil, so understanding the kingdom of God will produce in us a bountiful harvest of abundant life.

Read Psalm 36:8–9; John 4:13–14; Revelation 21:6.

Questions:

What are the qualities and characteristics of water that make it a perfect analogy of kingdom understanding?

_____

_____

_____

How can you ensure this flow of "water" in your life?

_____

_____

Daniel's Visions

In Daniel 7, the prophet describes the four nations he saw earlier in Nebuchadnezzar's statue-dream as beasts emerging from the sea. The description and perspective are different, but the same nations are in view. Nebuchadnezzar's dream detailed Gentile world history from man's perspective, while Daniel perceived these "times of the Gentiles" from God's vantage point.

Like the four metals of the image in Daniel 2, the four beasts of chapter 7 represent four world empires. In a related vision, Daniel foretells forthcoming events and the climaxing conflict of the world's superpowers (ch. 8). Thus, the prophecies of Daniel 2, 7, and 8 parallel each other in their universal scope and specific sequence.

World Empire	Nebuchadnezzar's Dream Monument	Daniel's First Vision	Daniel's Second Vision
Babylon (606–538 B.C.)	Head of Gold (2:32, 37, 38)	Lion (7:4)	
Medo-Persia (538–331 B.C.)	Breast, arms of silver (2:32, 39)	Bear (7:5)	Ram (8:3, 4, 20)
Greece (331–146 B.C.)	Belly, thighs of brass (2:32, 39)	Leopard (7:6)	Goat with one horn (8:5–8, 21)
			Four horns (8:8, 22)
			Little horn (8:9–14)
Rome (146 B.C.–A.D. 476)	Legs of iron Feet of iron and clay (2:33, 40, 41)	Strong beast (7:7, 11, 19, 23)	

Daniel's First Vision

Daniel's vision in chapter 7 is actually in four distinct parts. The scene is one of a great storm breaking forth on the "Great Sea," resulting in the emergence of four great beasts from the sea.

Daniel's vision shows human history in turmoil. "Four" is a number that is often used in reference to the things of this earth: "four seasons," "four corners," etc. "Winds" in symbolic passages refer to wars, strife, demonic activity, and judgments from God. Finally, "beasts" are often seen in symbolic passages representing kingdoms and their rulers. Each beast, emerging from the sea, typifies a great world empire coming forth to run its course.

Probing the Depths

The "little horn" of verse 8 is said to persecute (literally "wear out") the saints of the Most High. This seems to suggest mental affliction and circumstantial aggravation more than bodily harm. (It is interesting to compare this with the sufferings during the Great Tribulation and the horns mentioned in Revelation 13 and 17.) This "horn" will arise on the political scene following the rise of the ten "kings" from the kingdom which will "devour the whole earth." When the "little horn" arises, he will manifest intense persecution of the "saints of the Most High," for "a time and times and half a time." This is another way of saying three and one-half years. (Note: Classical interpretation views this term to represent an indefinite, divinely controlled time period.) God's judgment will end the reign of this evil "king" and dominion will be returned to the "saints of the Most High."

Read Daniel 7:8, 20–22; Revelation 7:4–17; 12:13–17.

Questions:

How may we apply Daniel 7:21 and 22 to our own spiritual warfare?

_____

_____

_____

What does this passage of Scripture reveal about satan's strategy towards all believers?

_____

_____

_____

How can it prepare us for spiritual adversity?

_____

_____

_____

The Kingdom of God

Read Daniel 7:9–14.

This passage links the four Gentile world powers with a literal, earthly kingdom of God, which follows them. The term "the Ancient of Days" refers to God the Father. The first occurrence of this term in verse 9 portrays God on His throne, judging the great world empires of Daniel's day. The second, in verse 13, is thought to be the Lord Jesus coming in the clouds of heaven to claim his rightful earthly inheritance from His Father, the Ancient of Days.

Read also Psalm 2:6–9; Luke 1:32; Mark 14:61, 62.

 Kingdom Life—*Possess the Kingdom*

Daniel's prophecy in chapter 7 spans the spiritual struggle covering the ages through Messiah's First and Second Coming. It also uses two terms important to understanding biblical truth of the kingdom of God: "dominion" and "possess." Dominion means to govern or prevail. Dominion will be in the hands of world powers until the Coming of the Son of Man, at which time it is taken by Him forever. But an interim struggle is seen between the First and Second Coming of Messiah. During this season the saints "possess" (meaning "to hold on" or "to occupy") the kingdom. This communicates a process of long struggle as the redeemed (saints) "possess" what they have received.

Read Daniel 7:21, 22.

Questions:

What pivotal event is predicted in the words "until the Ancient of Days came, and a judgment was made in favor of the saints?"

✎_____

_____

_____

What does it mean to "possess the kingdom?"

✎_____

_____

_____

How should this impact your life today?

✎ _____

_____

_____

_____

_____

Daniel's Second Vision

Read Daniel 8.

Two years after Daniel's visions of the four beasts, he saw another vision which gave additional information on some key questions. In the vision of Daniel 8:1–14, Daniel is taken to the palace at Shushan (or Susa), the winter capital of the Persian kings, about 230 miles east of Babylon. There he sees a battle between a two-horned ram and a one-horned goat.

 Behind the Scenes

The breaking of the notable horn in verse 8 was a reference to the untimely death of Alexander The Great in 323 B.C. at the apex of his strength. His kingdom was divided among his four generals, Lysimachus, Cassander, Seleucus and Ptolemy, represented in Daniel's vision by the four horns which arose in place of Alexander.

Out of Syria, one portion of Alexander's divided kingdom, came Antiochus IV, surnamed Epiphanes (Greek "God manifest"). He persecuted the Jews and profaned their temple, becoming known as the Old Testament Antichrist.

Antiochus attacked Jerusalem, killing or selling into slavery 90,000 men, women, and children. Under his pagan influence, the temple of God was dedicated to Jupiter Olympus. He used harlots in the temple to celebrate pagan feasts and forbade the observance of the Sabbath, the reading of Scripture, and circumcision.

Historians pinpoint the date Antiochus Epiphanes' ended sacrifices in the Jewish temple in Jerusalem as September, 171 B.C. On December 15, 168 B.C. he desecrated the temple by sacrificing a sow on the altar of the temple in what the Jews termed "the abomination of desolation." A Jewish revolt followed (described in two Apocryphal books, 1 and 2 Maccabees).

In December, 165 B.C., the Jewish patriots cleansed and rededicated the temple Antiochus had defiled. It is interesting to note that working backwards 2,300 days (Daniel 8:14), one arrives at the season in 171 B.C. when Antiochus began his harassment of the Jews.

The celebration of this cleansing of the temple later became a Jewish holiday known as the Feast of Dedication (John 10:22). Today it is known as Hanukkah and the Feast of Lights.

Read Daniel 8:14–15.

Questions:

How long will the "little horn" do away with the daily sacrifices in the temple in Jerusalem? Convert the answer into years, months and days.

✎ _____

_____

_____

_____

Compare this with the time period mentioned in Revelation 12:14. What is significant in this comparison?

✎ _____

_____

_____

_____

_____

The Interpretation

Read Daniel 8:15—27.

Antiochus Epiphanes may have been a historical "little horn," but there is yet a prophetical "little horn" (the Antichrist) who will do all his forerunner did and much more.

Read Revelation 12, 13, and 19; Daniel 8:9–20, 23–27.

Questions:

What similarities can you find in reference to the "little horn?"

✎_____

_____

_____

_____

Kingdom Life—*Seek to Understand*

Daniel's weighty spiritual experiences depleted him physically. He faithfully reported all that he saw, but had no means of understanding. Unlike us, Daniel did not have the completed Scriptures with which to derive understanding. God has given us His Word and the Holy Spirit enables us to unveil the meaning of many aspects of future events. God will lead you to grasp much of what He has revealed when seek to understand.

Read Revelation 1:3.

Questions:

A blessing is attached to reading biblical prophecy and "keeping" its truths.

✎_____

_____

_____

_____

_____

Why do you believe this is so?

✎_____

_____

_____

_____

_____

What blessings await those who will read and respond?

✎_____

_____

_____

_____

_____

_____

_____

Record Your Thoughts

All biblical truth, including prophecy, is intended to make the believer a mature person, fully equipped for good works (2 Timothy 3:16, 17). Before going further, pause for a few minutes and pray for the Holy Spirit to apply what you have studied thus far to your own life. Now list as many practical insights and applications as you can.

✎_____

_____

_____

_____

_____

_____

_____

SESSION SIX

The Preparation

Daniel 9:1–27

Kingdom Key—*Pray Without Ceasing*

1 Thessalonians 5:16–21 "Rejoice always, pray without ceasing, in everything give thanks; for this is the will of God in Christ Jesus for you. Do not quench the Spirit. Do not despise prophecies. Test all things; hold fast what is good."

Although Paul speaks here of prophecy as it is manifested in the church, this directive is no less true when considering the prophetic elements of Scripture. We should not shun them nor shy away from the attempt to understand.

We should, however, guard against receiving interpretation of these prophetic books from sources not wholly grounded on the Word of God. Scriptural accuracy is the sure test for all that is "good."

Above all, we must ask God for wisdom and listen closely as He leads us to understanding. Prayer is never more important than when we seek to discern the deeper meanings of God's Word.

Read 2 Timothy 3:16–17.

Questions:

What can be gained by studying biblical prophecy?

_____

_____

How can the truths contained be applied to your life today?

_____

_____

_____

Kingdom Life—*Repentance Allows Us to Receive*

Read Daniel 9.

Daniel had been in exile for over 70 years. In his old age, he studied Scripture and sought the Lord to find out when the Jewish captivity in Babylon would be completed. He longed for the fulfillment of God's gracious promises to Israel and entered into a time of concentrated prayer and fasting on behalf of his nation.

Although God had revealed much to Daniel, his response teaches us that the appropriate reaction to prophecy is often penitent prayer. Daniel pleaded with God for His nation, asking forgiveness and mercy.

Prophecy is not meant to be used for escapism nor a distraction from current ministry. It is, instead, a high and holy motivation for the present. God the Father, Judge of heaven and earth, calls us to holiness, that we may escape the wrath to come. Sensitive understanding of prophecy prompts personal repentance and intercession for others.

Read 1 Thessalonians 1:9–10; Psalm 51:17.

Questions:

How can the Spirit of prophecy elicit a penitent response?

_____

_____

_____

_____

_____

When have you experienced this?

_____

_____

_____

_____

_____

What was the result?

_____

_____

_____

The Seventy-Week Prophecy

Read Daniel 9:20–27.

In response to Daniel's penitent prayer and fasting, God sent His archangel Gabriel, giving Daniel an enigmatic answer that is one of the most critical prophetic passages in Scripture. Some of the predicted events have since been fulfilled with literal precision, and others—which are yet to come—provide the framework for the end times.

Probing the Depths

The following chart from *The Believer's Study Bible* displays a dispensational understanding of Daniel's seventy weeks:

The Prophecy of Seventy Weeks (490 Years)

Decree of Artaxerxes to Nehemiah—March 14, 445 B.C.		Presentation of Messiah as Prince—April 6, A.D. 32	Covenant of Antichrist with Israel		Return of Messiah to Establish Kingdom of God
v. 25 Sixty-nine Weeks (483 Years)		v. 26 Gap of Time	v. 27 Seventieth Week		
(Seven Weeks) 49 Years to Complete Rebuilding of Jerusalem	(Sixty-two Weeks= 434 Years)	Messiah Cut Off—A.D. 33 / Jerusalem and Sanctuary Destroyed—A.D. 70	3½ Years / Image of Antichrist in Temple	3½ Years Desolation by Antichrist / Six Purposes v. 24	

Students of the classical (non-dispensational) approach to prophetic interpretation do not view the "seventy weeks" literally, as referring precisely to 490 years. Adherents note that nowhere are the "weeks" (literally "sevens") said to be years. Instead, such students understand Daniel's use of "seventy weeks" in much the same way as they understand Jesus' use of "seventy times seven" when He instructs Peter to forgive freely (Matthew 18:21, 22). Students of the classical view of prophecy see Daniel's use of "seventy weeks" with much the same meaning; referring to a very long, indefinite period in which Israel is punished for her transgressions.

Word Wealth—*Messiah*

Messiah: *mashiach* (mah-shee-ahch); Strong's #4899: Anointed one, messiah. Found 39 times in the Old Testament, *mashiach* is derived from the verb *mashach*, "to anoint," "to consecrate by applying the holy anointing oil to an individual." *Mashiach* describes the high priest (Leviticus 4:3, 16) and anointed kings, such as Saul (2 Samuel 1:14) and David (2 Samuel 19:21; Psalm 18:50). In Psalms and in Daniel *mashiach* is particularly used for David's anointed heir, the king of Israel and ruler of all nations (see Psalms 2:2; 28:8; Daniel 9:25, 26). When the earliest followers of Jesus spoke of Him, they called Him Jesus the Messiah, or in Hebrew, *Yeshua ha-Mashiach*. "Messiah" or "Anointed One" is *Christos* in Greek and is the origin of the English form "Christ." Whenever the Lord is called "Jesus Christ," He is being called "Jesus the Messiah."

Behind the Scenes

Five temples are significant in the Jewish story:

1. **Solomon's temple,** (c. 1000 B.C.), symbol of Israel's glorious past;
2. **Zerubbabel's temple,** (c. 536 B.C.), a vastly inferior structure constructed by the Jews upon their return from the Babylonian captivity;
3. **Herod's temple,** begun around 19 B.C., to replace Zerubbabel's building. It was a magnificent edifice in service in Jesus' day, but destroyed by Titus in A.D. 70;
4. **Antichrist's temple,** built either before or during the early part of the first 3½ years of the tribulation, but due to be destroyed by the final earthquake before Jesus returns;
5. **Jesus Christ's temple,** built at the beginning of the millennium for Jesus' 1,000-year reign on earth."

Read 1 Corinthians 6:19; Hebrews 9:11–12.

Questions:

Why are we referred to as the "temple" of the Holy Spirit?

_____

_____

_____

What is the tabernacle "not made with hands"?

_____

_____

_____

In light of these two Scripture passages, what can we learn about our relationship with the Lord and our place in the kingdom?

_____

_____

_____

 Kingdom Extra

Read Daniel 9:26–27.

This final period of the "times of the Gentiles" is projected by futurists to begin when the Antichrist makes a covenant to protect Israel for a seven-year period (Isaiah 28:14–17). The first half of that time (42 months; Revelation 13:1–5) will be known to the Jews as "the beginning of sorrows" (Matthew 24:8). It will be characterized by conquest, war, famine, persecution, and death (Matthew 24:6–12; Revelation 6:1–8), as the Antichrist gathers a coalition of nations under his power (Revelation 13:3–5).

However, in the middle of Daniel's Seventieth Week (after 3½ years), the Antichrist will change his stance toward the Jews and demand that they worship him. This is the "abomination of desolation" to which Daniel and Paul refer (Daniel 9:27; 2 Thessalonians 2:2–4). It is followed by the period known as the "Great Tribulation" (Matthew 24:21, 29; Mark 13:19, 24; Revelation 7:14). It will include the desecration of the temple, great persecution of Israel, and the more severe judgments of the Tribulation period as God pours out His wrath (Revelation 6:17).

The final seven-year period concludes "after the tribulation of those days" with the Second Coming of Jesus, the Messiah (Matthew 24:29–31; Revelation 19:11–21). Following those events, Jesus will set up His kingdom and reign with His saints on earth for 1,000 years (Revelation 20:4–6), and then for all eternity with a new heaven, a new earth, and a new Jerusalem (Revelation 21).

Note: Classical interpreters see the initial fulfillment of Daniel's prophetic sections in past historical events, with the ultimate fulfillment for many prophecies to be experienced at the end of this age.

Record Your Thoughts

Reread Daniel 9 paying close attention to what is revealed about Daniel as he seeks the Lord.

Questions:

What aspects of his character can you discern that enabled him to hear so clearly from the Lord?

✎_____

_____

_____

_____

Compare these to the fruit of the Spirit found in Galatians 5:22. How do we obtain this fruit?

✎_____

_____

_____

How does your prayer life compare to that of Daniel?

✎_____

_____

_____

_____

The Battle

Daniel 10:1–12:13

 Kingdom Key—*Take Your Stand*

Ephesians 6:13 "Therefore, take up the whole armor of God, that you may be able to withstand in the evil day, and having done all, to stand."

We are engaged in an active battle now, today, in every way. While some suggest that the viewpoint of a continuous aggressive struggle minimizes the accomplished victory of the Cross, it in fact asserts that victory all the more. All spiritual warfare waged today is victorious only on the basis of appropriating the provision of the Cross and Christ's blood. Personal faith that positions itself against evil and aggressive prayer warfare that assails the demonic strongholds are two distinct and complimentary facets of spiritual life. It is only through employing these two powerful weapons of faith that we are enabled to stand before the onslaught of the enemy. The warfare waged against the kingdom of God will not end until the day our Lord returns.

Read Ephesians 6:10–18.

Questions:

What promises did Jesus make regarding prayer?

_____

_____

In what ways does your prayer life fail to live up to the description of prayer warfare in Ephesians 6?

_____

_____

_____

How does this hinder your walk with the Lord?

✎ _____

_____

_____

_____

_____

_____

Word Wealth—*Withstand*

Withstand: Greek *anthistemi* (anth-is'-tay-mee): The word from which our term "antihistamine" is derived. From *anti,* which means "against" and *histemi* meaning "to cause to stand." The verb suggests vigorously opposing, bravely resisting, standing face-to-face against an adversary, standing your ground. Just as an antihistamine puts a block on histamine, *anthistemi* tells us that with the authority and spiritual weapons granted to us we can withstand evil forces.

Daniel Prepared Through Prayer

Read Daniel 10:1—12:13.

These passages contain one great unit of prophecy revealing world history in advance. Two years before this final vision given to Daniel in 538 B.C., the Persian King, Cyrus, issued a decree allowing some of the exiled Jews to return to Jerusalem to rebuild the house of God (2 Chronicles 36:22, 23; Ezra 1; Isaiah 44:28). Daniel had either been told of, or senses in his spirit, the opposition and resistance his people would face in rebuilding the temple in Jerusalem.

Daniel's heart was heavy and he diligently sought the Lord through prayer and fasting. Daniel 10:2, 3 reveals the prophet's temporary abstinence from certain foods, which reflects what some call a "Daniel's fast." He went without pastries, meat, and wine as a discipline to express spiritual mourning. Some have suggested that this three-week fast was during the period of the Passover Feast.

Read Daniel 9:3–20; Psalm 69:10–36.

Questions:

What is your understanding of the purpose and intent of fasting?

✎ _____

_____

_____

How have you experienced God's power manifested as a result of fasting?

✎ _____

_____

_____

How can fasting enable you to stand strong before the weapons of the enemy?

✎ _____

_____

_____

Behind the Scenes

Passover was originally a feast celebrated by those about to be delivered by their direct obedience to the covenant God; it served as the final dynamic proof of God's presence and protective care. Its continued celebration by all the congregation of Israel serves as a memorial for those who were delivered and their offspring.

It is celebrated in the month of Nisan (also called Abib, March–April), and marks the new year because it signifies the beginning of Israel's new life as a people. It is characterized by selecting a lamb, which is sacrificed four days later and eaten as part of a major commemorative meal. A feast of hope and life, the Passover represents deliverance and new beginnings; in many of its elements, it is a type of Christ our Redeemer, the Lamb of God.

Read Exodus 12:1–14.

Kingdom Life—*The Power of a Humble Heart*

Daniel's faith was such that, he continuously maintained an attitude of surrender and humility. He longed to hear from God and sought Him tenaciously, recognizing that only through the Lord could he find direction and peace. Daniel's humble spirit and desperate pleas in prayer paved the way for God to reveal powerful messages of future events to him.

Read Daniel 10:11–12; 2 Corinthians 12:9–10; James 4:10.

Questions:

What is your understanding of the meaning of humility?

_____

_____

_____

How can this attitude pave the way to victorious living in Christ?

_____

_____

_____

In what ways is humility exhibited in your own life?

_____

_____

_____

The Heavenly Visitation

Read Daniel 10:10–21.

The heavenly being that appeared to Daniel bears great similarity to the description of Jesus in Revelation 1:12–16. Daniel's reaction to this holy presence is much the same as is recorded of others who have found themselves in the presence of God.

An additional personality seems to be introduced in Daniel 10:10. This being described a battle with the prince of Persia. This is one of the clearest Old Testament examples that demonic armies oppose God's purposes. It also provides insight that earthly struggles often reflect what is happening in the heavenlies, and prayer with fasting may affect the outcome of these spiritual battles. It would appear that the demonic world is exceedingly active in the affairs of nations and national issues. The conflict is *in* the spiritual realm, yet it is *expressed through* political, military, and other realms.

Joining in this battle is Michael who is identified in Scripture as a senior angel. The exact nature of this particular conflict is not stated.

Read Isaiah 6:1–5; Luke 5:8; Revelation 1:17.

Questions:

Have you ever had an experience in which you had a similar reaction to the Lord's presence?

_____

_____

_____

Why do you believe this is so?

_____

_____

_____

Kingdom Extra

This text, as well as other examples in Scripture, make it clear that "principalities and powers" in the heavenly realm war continually and victories and defeats in this realm determine earthly events. Unfortunately, in today's church, believers become too easily detoured, "wrestling" with human adversaries instead of prayerfully warring against the invisible works of hell behind the scenes. The church must recognize that its corporate assignment is to prayer warfare, in order to see evil vanquished and the will of God advanced.

Read Matthew 16:19; 2 Corinthians 10:4; Ephesians 6:12.

Questions:

How does your prayer life reflect your understanding of your involvement in the war in the heavenlies?

✎_____

_____

_____

_____

With this truth in mind, how might this affect the timing of answers to prayer?

✎_____

_____

_____

_____

What role does perservering prayer have in spiritual conflict?

✎_____

_____

_____

_____

What can happen if we do not assume our role as intercessors?

✎_____

_____

_____

_____

Prophecies Concerning Persia and Greece

Read Daniel 11:2–35.

Daniel 11 appears to prophesy the plight of the Jews and the suffering they will endure in the centuries to follow. They will continue in danger throughout modern history and until the end of the Great Tribulation.

From a twenty-first-century vantage point all prophecy in Daniel up to Daniel 11:35 can be related to well-known events of ancient history. For instance, the dreams Daniel interpreted in chapters 2, 7, and 8 overlap in meaning and relate to features of the Babylonian, Medo-Persian, Greek, and Roman world empires.

Daniel 11:2–4 describes again Alexander's rise and the future division of his empire after he was cut off in his prime at age thirty-three. Daniel 11:5–20 predicts the intrigue and struggles between Egypt and Syria right up until the time of Antiochus Epiphanes (c. 175–164 B.C.). Daniel 11:21–35 describes the outrageous actions of Antiochus and ultimately of the final enemy of God's people, the Antichrist.

The Time of the End

Read Daniel 11:36—12:13.

The remaining verses of Daniel reveal the events immediately preceding time's end and our Lord's return. These verses reveal the brutality and cruelty of the Antichrist, referred to here as "the king of the North. We are given insight into the Antichrist's obsession with war and military force. (Read also Ezekiel 38:8, 9, 11 and 16.)

As fierce as the Antichrist may be, he will not prevail against the true Christ, the Anointed One of God. His eventual end is prophesied in Revelation 19:11–21.

 Kingdom Life—*By His Grace, We Shall Stand*

The agonizing days of God's wrath, predicted in Daniel 9:27 and revealed further in Revelation 16, will be so severe that, except for the restraining work of the archangel Michael (Daniel 12:1), Israel's guardian angel, the remaining human race might face annihilation.

Daniel distinguishes two phases of a future resurrection of the dead. Some will be resurrected to everlasting life and some to shame and everlasting contempt or abhorrence. The former most likely refers to the "last days" resurrection of the remnant of Jewish martyrs (Revelation 6:9; Matthew 10:22, 23) which precedes the Great White Throne Judgment after the Millennium. (Read also Revelation 20:4–6.)

Daniel is ordered to conceal and close up the book until "the time of the end." When the end time comes, the church will have a greater historical perspective to understand prophecy. In the view of many, since Israel regained control of its homeland (1948), and of the city of Jerusalem (1967), we have a much clearer perspective on prophecy because the end time is significantly nearer than before.

Read Matthew 24:22; Revelation 12:7–9.

Questions:

What insight do these Scriptures give you into the heart of the Lord where the end of time is concerned?

_____

_____

_____

_____

How does this aspect of God's nature affect your life today?

_____

_____

_____

_____

_____

Kingdom Extra

Throughout the history of the church, many Christians have become so consumed with the future realities that they have neglected their present responsibilities. For instance, during the first century A.D. believers in Thessalonica heard that Christ had already come and established His kingdom on earth. Some of them used this news to excuse themselves from work and to engage in gossip. After challenging their response to this unfounded message, the apostle Paul corrected their theology, reminding them of what he had taught them about the last days.

Read 2 Thessalonians 2:2–13.

Question:

Search the Internet or other reference materials and make note of the times in history when believers have pinned their hopes on a specific date. What was the result of their erroneous belief?

✎_____

_____

_____

Record Your Thoughts

Questions:

How are you handling your own priorities until the end of time?

✎_____

_____

_____

With the prospect of these awful afflictions and challenging circumstances near "the time of the end," how are the wise and righteous to respond? (2 Thessalonians 1:10).

✎_____

_____

_____

If tomorrow was the day the "great tribulation" was to begin, would you be able to stand?

✎_____

_____

_____

What steps can you take today to prepare yourself to stand strong, regardless of the trials that come?

✎_____

_____

_____

ADDITIONAL OBSERVATIONS

Session Eight

The Call

Revelation 1:1–3:32

 Kingdom Key—Be a Partaker of Blessing

2 Peter 1:3–4 ". . . His divine power has given to us all things that pertain to life and godliness, through the knowledge of Him who called us by glory and virtue, by which have been given to us exceedingly great and precious promises, that through these you may be partakers of the divine nature, having escaped the corruption that is in the world through lust."

The incarnate life of Christ has made available to believers His "exceedingly great and precious promises." These promises surely include the Lord's Second Coming, the establishment of a new heaven and earth, and entrance into Christ's kingdom. But they would also recommend our bold acceptance in Christ of all the promises of God. Christ is the fulfiller and fulfillment of all the promises of God because He is their sum and substance. The purpose of the promises is that we may be sharers of a deep spiritual union with Christ, and thereby of the blessings and benefits of that relationship. The promises are also an incentive to godliness, because to share in His fullness now, as well as future glory, we must renounce "the corruption that is in the world."

Read 2 Corinthians 1:20; Matthew 28:18–20; 2 Peter 2:1–4.

Questions:

What are the promises of God to believers? List as many as you can find.

_____

_____

_____

In what way do those promises affect you today?

✎ _____

_____

_____

_____

_____

_____

The Revelation of Jesus Christ

The Book of Revelation is an "unveiling" of supernatural wisdom and destiny. It is typically apocalyptic (Greek word, *apokalupsis* meaning "disclosure" or "uncovering") in form, revealing the future through figurative description and symbolism. What the Book of Daniel is to the Old Testament, the Book of Revelation is to the New Testament.

From the beginning of this book we note that this revelation is of Jesus Christ Himself. It is an unveiling of His plans for His creation, especially His church.

 Kingdom Life—*A Promised Blessing*

This book of Scripture is unique in that it contains a promise of blessing to its readers: read Revelation 1:3.

The Greek word *makarios*, translated as "blessed," (happy, fulfilled, and satisfied) is found seven times in Revelation (1:3; 14:13; 16:15; 19:9; 20:6; 22:7, 14). It is the familiar word used by our Lord in the Beatitudes in Matthew 5 and Luke 6, where it indicates not only the character traits that are blessed, but also the nature of that which is the highest good.

The Lord pronounces those who *read, hear,* and *keep* the words of this prophecy will have inner satisfaction because God dwells within them, not necessarily because of favorable circumstances. The blessing of God can bring peace in the middle of turmoil and the storms of life.

Questions:

In what ways is your life blessed?

✎_____

_____

_____

_____

What future blessings are promised to believers?

✎_____

_____

_____

_____

The Risen Christ

Read Revelation 1:13–17.

Many believers only think of the suffering Jesus hanging on the cross. But we serve a mighty, resurrected, victorious Lord. If we had a true glimpse of Christ's majesty, holiness, and power, perhaps we too would fall down and worship Him "in spirit and in truth." Perhaps the brilliance of His glory would reveal areas and aspects of our lives for which we need quick and genuine repentance!

The Lord Jesus came from heaven to earth to redeem mankind. He willingly left His royal glory behind to become a servant to His creatures on earth. But now, having risen from the grave, He has returned to heaven and John shares with us his glimpse of Godly glory.

Read Philippians 2:6–11; John 14:1–4.

Questions:

How can "this mind be in you?"

✎_____

_____

_____

_____

What other Scriptures can you locate that give insight into the glory of the risen Lord?

_____

_____

_____

What promises are ours because Jesus has returned to the Father?

_____

_____

_____

Kingdom Extra

The seven golden lampstands represent the seven churches located along a major Roman postal route. These churches are listed in the order in which a messenger would reach the towns, making a semicircular sweep from Ephesus. The symbolism of lampstands suggests that the churches are lights in a dark world.

The symbolism is an apt one in that a lamp contains oil and a wick and can continuously burn and give light as long as its oil is replenished and its wick consistently trimmed. The significance of this symbolism is clear concerning spiritual renewal and holy living in the local church and in "the temple of the Holy Spirit"—ourselves.

In the message to the church at Ephesus, Jesus said that He "walks in the midst of the seven golden lampstands" (2:1). This seems to suggest an **intimate concern** and **intense care** for the local assemblies of believers. He is the One who fills (and refills) the oil, and trims (and even replaces) the wick.

Questions:

What does this say to us about diversity in forms of worship and styles of services?

_____

_____

_____

What could this analogy suggest about spiritual renewal and leadership in a local church?

✎ _____

_____

_____

_____

Do you need more "oil in your lamp"? Do you need your wick trimmed? Are you "burned out"?

✎ _____

_____

_____

Kingdom Extra

The Seven Churches of the Apocalypse *(Revelation 1:20)*

(From *The Spirit Filled Life Bible, New King James Version,* page 1961. Used by permission.)

	Commendation	Criticism	Instruction	Promise
Ephesus 2:1–7	Rejects evil, perseveres, has patience	Love for Christ no longer fervent	Do the works you did at first	The tree of life
Smyrna (2:8–11)	Gracefully bears suffering	None	Be faithful until death	The crown of life
Pergamos (2:12–17)	Keeps the faith of Christ	Tolerates immorality, idolatry, and heresies	Repent	Hidden manna and a stone with a new name
Thyatira (2:18–29)	Love, service, faith, patience is greater than at first	Tolerates cult of idolotry and immorality	Jusgment coming; keep the faith	Rule over nations and receive morning star
Sardis (3:1–6)	Some have kept the faith	A dead church	Repent; strengthen what remains	Faithful honored and clothed in white
Philadelphia (3:7–13)	Perseveres in the faith	None	Keep the faith	A place in God's presence, a new name, and the New Jerusalem
Laodicea (3:14–22)	None	Indifferent	Be zealous and repent	Share Christ's throne

The Letters to the Seven Churches

The Revelation was addressed and sent to the Seven Churches of Asia Minor (now the country of Turkey). The churches were specific congregations in John's day, but they also are representative of similar types of churches, regardless of place or time.

In these epistles the risen Lord administers His church. Each letter includes:

- an accusation or commendation,
- a call or directive, and
- a threat or a promise.

Though they were *actual churches*, they also seem to have been selected as *parable churches* to give heavenly instruction throughout all generations of the church (Revelation 2:7, 11, 17, 29; 3:6, 13, 22).

 Kingdom Life—*Make Love Your Aim*

Read Revelation 2:1–7.

The church at Ephesus had been initially taught by Paul, and tradition holds that the apostle John made his residence there both before and after his imprisonment on the Isle of Patmos. Though well-taught, knowledgeable, and diligent in their observance of orthodox teaching, the church at Ephesus had become devoid of love. The spiritual vitality springing from love for the Lord had degenerated into orthodox routine.

The Lord exhorts the Ephesian church to repent. He tells them that He will "remove" their "lampstand." Although this seems to threaten extinction, it must be remembered that a congregation may continue to exist without being light in the darkness.

Read 1 Corinthians 14:1; 1 John 2:5–8; 3:14–16.

Questions:

What does it mean to leave your "first love?"

Although this passage refers to a local church, what can you glean from Jesus' words that can apply to your own life?

_____

_____

_____

Does the world know you have passed from death to life, by watching your life?

_____

_____

_____

 Kingdom Life—Be Faithful

Read Revelation 2:8–11.

Another leading congregation in Asia Minor was located in the town of Smyrna, about forty miles north of Ephesus. Of the seven cities addressed in Revelation 2 and 3, this is the only one which exists today; it is the modern Turkish town of Izmir. In the first century it was a wealthy seaport, and a place of advanced culture for that time.

Christ prophesied of a time of intense future persecution for the believers in Smyrna. Satan, He said, would actually deliver many of them into prison. However, He urged them to be faithful and promised them "the crown of life" which is symbolic of the joy of eternal life.

Probing the Depths

Who can deny that we—as Christians—have troubles, pressures, or "tribulations"? The word in Revelation 1:9 which is translated "tribulations" (Greek *thlipsis*) was also used in classical Greek to describe the way the Romans would torture someone by applying the pressure of heavy stones to the chest of a criminal. This heavy pressure had the effect of slowly mashing the individual to death.

Do you have problems that are slowly "mashing" you down to the point you feel you can't take it any more? Jesus says He "knows" all about our afflictions, our deep distresses, our pressing problems. He knows and cares! He knows our present pressures and future trials as well. His Word assures us of final victory.

Read Romans 8:31–39; James 1:12; 1 Peter 5:4; 2 Timothy 3:12; Romans 8:35–39; 2 Corinthians 5:1–8.

Questions:

According to the Scripture portions above, what is the reason for trial and what should be your reaction?

✎_____

_____

_____

How do you react to pressure and trial?

✎_____

_____

_____

Kingdom Life—*Don't Compromise*

Read Revelation 2:12–17.

The church at Pergamos was located in the oldest province and the official seat of the Roman government. It had become a doctrinally compromising church. While they had refused to deny Jesus as Lord in the face of persecution, they had begun following teachings and doctrines that were leading them into idolatry and immorality.

Jesus promised three things to those who would repent:

1. **Hidden manna:** Jewish apocryphal mythology maintained that the pot of manna in the ark (see Exodus 16:4, 31–34) was hidden by Jeremiah, or taken by an angel to heaven, at the time of the destruction of Jerusalem in 586 B.C., where it would remain until the Messiah should come. Jesus is the "true bread from heaven."

2. **A white stone**—Juries entered their verdicts by casting a stone in an urn: black for guilty and white for acquittal.
3. **A new name**—This refers to the imputed character of Christ.

To avoid compromise and overcome sinful temptation, mature believers must feed on the meat of the Word. It is the Word of truth and the Spirit of God which make us able to discern unsound doctrine and unwholesome conduct.

Read Hebrews 12:6; 5:12–14.

Questions:

How can we avoid being "narrow minded" and yet not tolerate sin?

✎ _____

_____

_____

What compromises do you find yourself tempted to make in your walk with the Lord?

✎ _____

_____

_____

Kingdom Life—*Maintain Purity*

Read Revelation 2:18–29.

Thyatira was about thirty-five miles southeast of Pergamos. It had been founded nearly 400 years before by Alexander the Great. The church of that city was in serious trouble, caused by the demands of the many trade guilds (such as tanners, potters, etc.). These fraternal associations frequently sponsored ceremonial feasts, characterized by immoral conduct, and celebrated with food "sacrificed" to some pagan deity, possibly the guild's patron god.

The Thyatiran letter is all about Christian life and witness in a permissive society. While eating food sacrificed to idols is not an issue for us in Western society, the principle here is important and relevant to Christians today.

Question:

Do you take your standards from contemporary moral values or from God's unchanging Word?

✎ _____

_____

_____

 Kingdom Life—*Wise Choices*

Some areas of our lives present situations that are not directly spoken to in Scripture. Consider the following principles and questions to help in developing your own personal convictions. Objectively apply *all* the following "guidelines for gray areas" to a given issue before deciding if the matter in question is right or wrong for you.

1. **Profit** (1 Corinthians 6:12). Ask the questions: 'Is it good for me?' 'Will it add a plus quality to my life?'
2. **Control** (1 Corinthians 6:12). Ask the questions: 'Will it get control of me, or will it lessen Christ's control of me?'
3. **Ownership** (1 Corinthians 6:19, 20). Consider the questions: 'As God's property, can I justify this activity? Is this activity befitting an ambassador of Jesus Christ?'
4. **Influence** (1 Corinthians 8:9, 12, 13). Consider: 'Could this action negatively influence any of my friends or cause them to stumble?'
5. **Testimony** (Colossians 4:5). Now consider: 'How will my testimony be affected if I participate in this activity?'
6. **Thanksgiving** (Colossians 3:17). Reflect on this question: 'When I come home from this activity, can I thank God for it with a clear conscience?'
7. **Love** (Romans 14:13–15). As the final question ask: 'Am I willing to limit my liberties, in loving consideration of another?'

That Woman Jezebel

Jezebel was the wicked, idolatrous wife of King Ahab (1 Kings 16:29–31; 18:4; 19:2; 2 Kings 9:22). Her name is used here symbolically for false teaching which was leading people into literal and spiritual fornication. "Jezebel's" fate is one of judgment as she leads others into the "depths of satan" or the deceitful snare of heretical teaching.

But Jesus promises that all who stand firm in their faith and hold to His truth will share in His triumph over all evil and in His messianic rule which was inaugurated at His First Coming. Above all, the over-comer will receive Jesus Himself, "the morning star," which heralds the dawn of a New Day and is our ultimate reward.

Read Romans 6:1–23.

Questions:

In what ways do experience your "freedom from sin?"

_____

_____

_____

_____

In what ways do you experience sin's deceitful power?

_____

_____

_____

_____

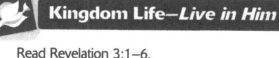

Kingdom Life—*Live in Him*

Read Revelation 3:1–6.

Thirty miles southeast of Thyatira and fifty miles due east of Smyrna, was Sardis, a city of luxury, apathy and licentious religiosity.

This letter to the church in Sardis departs from the pattern set by Christ in the preceding letters and we find no praise as Christ addresses this church. Instead, harsh evaluation is immediate. This spiritually weak congregation is living off the accolades of their past spiritual service to Christ. But Jesus declares that this church is "dead."

That which is dead is inflexible and unresponsive. Death's heart is cold and its eyes blind. Death is that state in which God is not. Yet Jesus has won the victory over death and offers life to those who will open their eyes, recognize His sacrifice and Lordship, follow the principles of the kingdom, be steadfast and firm in their faith, and repent of their sin. Those who demonstrate spiritual sincerity are rewarded by Christ's daily companionship ("walk with me") and consequent purity. To these He promises robes of righteousness, victorious joy, and the certainty of eternal life.

Read John 10:10; Romans 6:1–4.

Questions:

Do you experience abundant life in the Lord?

_____

_____

_____

Why do you believe this is so?

_____

_____

_____

Word Wealth—*Repent*

Repent: Greek *metanoeo* (met-an-ah-eh´-oh); Strong's #3340: From meta, "after," and noeo, "to think." The first call of the kingdom is to repentance. The implications of biblical repentance are threefold: 1) renunciation and reversal, 2) submission and teachability, and 3) continual malleability. There is no birth into the kingdom without hearing the call to salvation, renouncing one's sin and turning from sin toward Christ the Savior (Acts 3:19).

There is no growth in the kingdom without obedience to Jesus' commandments and a childlike responsiveness as a disciple of Jesus, yielding to the teaching of God's Word (James 1:21–25).

There is no lifelong increase of fruit as a citizen of the kingdom without a willingness to accept the Holy Spirit's correction and guidance (Ephesians 4:30).

Kingdom Life—*Be Faithful*

Philadelphia means "brotherly love." it was a faithful church in a small town that was established to be a center of Greek culture. The town was renowned for its surrounding vineyards but subject to frequent earthquakes.

The letter to Philadelphia makes reference to the "key of David" which symbolizes authority (Isaiah 22:22; Revelation 5:5; 22:16) and to "an open door" which is set before the people by the authority of Christ Jesus Himself. Two interpretations of this "open door" are possible. First, it may be the door to the eternal kingdom. Not only can Jesus open the door to that opportunity, He *is* the Door (John 10:7, 9).

Second, it may be the "door" of witness, service, and evangelistic opportunity. Philadelphia was described as the "gateway to the East." It was a center from which Greek culture was propagated. (See also 1 Corinthians 16:9; 2 Corinthians 2:12.)

This church is described as having "little strength." When we are weak, we must depend on the Lord. The temptation will be to deny, to distort, or dilute God's Word to accommodate our weakness or vulnerability. But Jesus said Philadelphia had shown biblical fidelity and had "kept My word, and not denied My name."

Read Philippians 2:12–16.

Questions:

Do you "hold fast" to the truth of God's word in the face of adversity?

_____

_____

_____

In what way do you experience God's word adding strength to you?

_____

_____

_____

The Promises

Jesus warns those who try to oppress His church and also encourages the believers by assuring that His return is eminent. He also encourages His church by promising that overcomers will become pillars in the temple of God. This refers to the common practice of honoring a notable citizen by erecting a pillar in a temple with his name inscribed. The Lord will so honor His faithful by permanently inscribing on them the name of God, the New Jerusalem, and Christ. This indicates identification with and possession by God, a spiritual citizenship, and a reflection of the character of Christ.

Probing the Depths—*Give Your Opinion*

Revelation 3:10 promises that Christ will keep believers "from the hour of trial," a promise whose specific reference has been debated by sincere Christian scholars and theologians. Regarding the timing of the rapture of the church, does this promise mean that believers will *escape from* the "trials" of the tribulation period, or that they will *endure through* the midst of them? Or, does "hour of trial" refer to that which was to come upon the Philadelphian church only?

The Greek phrase "keep from" (*tereo ek*) is used elsewhere only in John 17:15, where Christ prayed to the Father that He would "keep" believers from satan.

Does He mean to preserve them from attack by the Evil One, or preserve them *through* such attack? Explain your response.

What about the rest of verse 10? Does the promise apply to the entire seven-year period (Daniel's Seventieth Week) or to the last three and one-half years (the "Great Tribulation"), when the "hour of temptation" comes to the "whole world"? Explain your choice.

Kingdom Life—*Take a Stand*

Laodicea was an arrogant, self-sufficient, lukewarm church in an affluent city noted for being a center of banking and commerce. But they were a spiritually lethargic church. They desperately needed the grace that regenerates, the garments of Christ's righteousness, and Spirit-illuminated eyes of the heart.

Jesus apparently has greater patience for fiery hot fanaticism or icy cold formalism than for the lifelessness of Laodicea. It is not clear from Jesus' warning whether this lethargic church is in danger of losing their justification, but we certainly see from Jesus' words that nominal Christianity deprives us of the blessings of intimacy with Jesus.

Yet Jesus tells this complacent church that they may still "open the door" and enjoy intimate fellowship with Him. That He waits for the door to be opened shows the paradox of grace and personal responsibility.

Record Your Thoughts

Questions:

Which of the churches do you most relate to?

_____

_____

_____

_____

_____

_____

Have you ever experienced spiritual lethargy?

_____

_____

_____

What have you learned in this session that will enable you to walk more faithfully and effectively with the Lord?

_____

_____

_____

_____

_____

ADDITIONAL OBSERVATIONS

SESSION NINE

The Power

Revelation 4:1—8:1

Kingdom Key—*Press in to Worship*

John 4:23 "But the hour is coming, and now is, when the true worshippers will worship the Father in spirit and truth; for the Father is seeking such to worship Him.

In this section, we study the third and fourth divisions of John's Revelation: the *songs* of preparation, and the *seals* of judgment. Revelation 4 and 5 describe the awesome events the apostle saw concerning "things which must take place" in human history on earth prior to the judgments which are designed to deliver the planet from the control of the devil. John's heart was prepared for the pictures of fearful judgments by first seeing a vision of God's glory and triumph. It is important to perceive a principle here: all judgment is preceded by worship.

It is the believer's responsibility to discover how the Lord wants to be worshipped and to explore and cultivate a relationship with Him out of which sincere, Holy Spirit-enabled worship will flow. Jesus instructs us to worship in "spirit"—that is, alive through new birth and aglow with Holy Spirit enablement. This is not a mechanical, rote, or merely human activity but a dynamically capacitated spiritual action. "In truth" emphasizes biblical integrity joined to personal honesty, manifest in a heart of sincerity, a humble manner of transparency, and a relational integrity. Meaning and being what we say, as well as being spiritually energized in our worship, opens the way to that worship the Father seeks.

Read Psalms 29:1; 96; 1 Chronicles 16:23–36.

Questions:

David had the heart of a true worshipper. What does this mean?

_____

_____

How does your worship compare to that of David?

_____

_____

_____

What are some ways we can worship the Lord?

_____

_____

_____

Behind the Scenes

Many students of prophetic study understand the apostle John to be primarily following a method known as *discursive description* in trying to communicate his vision. He seems to be relating the big picture of what he saw, digressing from one topic to another, without any particular regard for arranging his presentation by a simple sequence of time. For instance, these seven seals seem to be overlapping and integrated judgments continuing throughout human history.

The Throne Room of Heaven

Read Revelation 4:1–11.

This passage offers the most complete picture of the throne of God in the Bible. This scene integrates the majesty of the Almighty, the court of His cherubim and elders, and the Lion/Lamb Redeemer. God is not described in form, but in terms of brilliance and glory.

To more clearly understand this passage, you must recognize the meanings of its elements:

1. **Jasper**—probably a diamond, suggesting purity or holiness.
2. **Sardius**—a deep red stone, picturing God's avenging wrath.
3. **Emerald**—a green stone, the dominant color in a rainbow which symbolizes mercy.
4. **Elders**—celestial representatives of all the redeemed, glorified and enthroned, who worship continuously.

5. **White robes**—symbolize purity.
6. **Crowns**—suggests victory and joy, not political authority.
7. **Sea of glass**—denotes the unapproachableness and majesty of God.
8. **Four Living Creatures**—are angelic beings who resemble Ezekiels' and Isaiah's vision of cherubim. They are the highest ranking celestial beings and represent all the vital forces of creation whose primary function is worship. The fact that they are "full of eyes" symbolizes unceasing watchfulness. Their identities are symbolized by different appearances: lion—courage, calf—strength, man—intelligence, eagle—speed; all in service to their Creator.

Read Ezekiel 1; Isaiah 6; Psalms 18; 82.

Questions:

What do these Scriptures impart as to the majesty of God?

_____

_____

_____

Why do you believe Scripture does not contain a description of God's form?

_____

_____

_____

Probing the Depths

The book of Revelation contains 20 passages, known as chorales, in which a large group extols the holiness, omnipotence and eternal nature of God. These passages hold the interpretation of many of the vision throughout Revelation. Locate each and make note of the truths they contain. This will greatly assist you in your quest to grasp the meaning and import of this incredible book.

Read through a few of the Psalms.

Questions:

How are the 20 chorales found in Revelation similar to the Psalms?

_____

_____

_____

Why do you believe this similarity exists?

_____

_____

_____

The Scroll

Read Revelation 5:1–7.

In this setting, God is holding a book or scroll in His right hand. It is sealed with seven seals, which represent and reveal the pending judgments which are to try those who live on the earth.

Some have likened this sealed scroll to a title deed to a piece of property which is about to be redeemed by a relative. The judgments are what is required to drive out the enemy who is in unlawful possession of it.

When Adam sinned he lost his inheritance of the earth (Genesis 1:26–28), it passed out of his hands into the possession of satan, and resulted in the disinheritance of all of Adam's seed. The forfeited title deed is now in God's hands and is awaiting ultimate redemption by Jesus. (See Leviticus 25:23–28 and compare with Jeremiah 32:6–15.)

Read Isaiah 54; John 1:29.

Questions:

What significance is it that the book is held in God's right hand?

_____

_____

_____

Why was a "Lion" proclaimed as being worthy to open the book, but it was a wounded "Lamb" which did so?

✎ _____

_____

_____

What is suggested by the fact that the Lamb was slain, but is living?

✎ _____

_____

_____

_____

When Jesus takes the book from His Father ("Him who sat on the throne"), He has the right to break its seals and claim the inheritance and dispossess the present claimant, satan. This event is the fulfillment of Daniel's vision of the "Ancient of Days" in Daniel 7:9–14.

Worthy Is the Lamb

Read Revelation 5:8–14.

The four living creatures and the twenty-four elders are the first to worship the Lamb. They are followed in praise and worship by myriads of angels and all the redeemed humanity in heaven. Finally, every created being ("in heaven and on the earth and under the earth and such as are in the sea") joins the cosmic chorus. Their great theme, in answer to the earlier quest (5:2, 3), is "Worthy is the Lamb."

Read Mark 16:15–18; Philippians 2:10–11.

Questions:

What does John's vision say to us about the fulfillment of the Great Commission?

✎ _____

_____

_____

_____

What was the predetermined purpose of this cosmic chorus?

✎ _____

_____

_____

Kingdom Key—*Worship His Majesty*

Read Revelation 5.

Every created thing responds with honor, glory, and blessing to the Lord (Revelation 5:13). Worship is the means of fulfilling the purpose of our common creation. As a royal priesthood the saints reign now with Christ on the earth by their worship, their prayers, and their witness in word and deed. This sense of praise is in progress now and throughout redemptive history.

Every created being joins the cosmic chorus and ascribes to the Lamb every attribute of God. All history is moving toward the predestined goal of the eventual and ultimate universal recognition of the lordship of Jesus Christ.

Read Philippians 2:10–11; Psalms 69:34; 109:30.

Questions:

David spoke of praising multitudes. Find other examples of this in the Psalms.

✎ _____

_____

_____

What is the result of praise to the Lord?

✎ _____

_____

_____

The Lamb, invested with all the authority to execute judgment, begins now to open the first four seals with His nail-pierced hands. What we see in this ever-intensifying series of seal judgments is what our Lord called the "beginning of sorrows" (Matthew 24:8).

The Seven Seals

Read Revelation 6:1—8:1.

The scroll cannot be unrolled until all seven seals are broken. The time of the eschatological (the biblical study of end times) fulfillment of the events of the first six seals is therefore best seen as corresponding to the time Jesus references as "the beginning of sorrows" (Matthew 24:8). This is thought by many to be the beginning of Daniel's Seventieth Week (Daniel 9:27). The Great Tribulation therefore begins with the events of the first trumpet (which corresponds to the events of the seventh seal; see 8:1). Zechariah's visions of the four horsemen who patrol the earth may have been creatively utilized here (see Zechariah 1:8–10; 6:1–7).

When the Lamb broke the first seal, the first living creature cried with a voice of thunder, "Come and see." The cry is not addressed to John, but to one of the "Four Horsemen of the Apocalypse" on their errand of judgment.

The First Seal

Many see the rider on the white horse as the symbol of international power politics in the form of military conquest. Others see the white horse as Christ continuing to move in triumph through His church during the throes of the events that follow the breaking of this seal, conquering through tribulation and to conquer ultimately over all (see 19:11–16).

Question:

What other Scriptures can you locate that would lead you to believe that Jesus is the "conqueror" on the white horse?

_____

_____

_____

Behind the Scenes

The Dispensationalist would see this rider, who symbolized political conquest, as the antichrist, who will come imitating Christ and claiming to be Him. (See Matthew 24:4, 5; John 5:43.)

Others would see this as descriptive of the delusion by which many antichrists have attempted to rule and deceive throughout church history (1 John 2:18). They understand Scripture to say that the visible church in a violent, unrepentant world will experience testing and tribulation along with the sinners. But God's sovereignty and promises provide a "sure and certain hope" for people of God's kingdom!

The Second Seal

The second living creature summoned the rider on a fiery red horse, who was granted to "take peace from the earth." This rider is the symbol of civil war and strife.

The Third Seal

The rider on the black horse is the symbol of economic disruption. The problem is not famine, but inflation and scarcity. The inflation will be so severe that a day's wages will purchase only about ⅛ as much as under normal conditions. The oil and wine is symbolic of luxury and likely means the famine is limited in scope and does not depict worldwide, rampant starvation.

The Fourth Seal

The next rider is named "Death." And "Hades" (not "Hell"), that region of departed spirits, figuratively follows afterward to consume Death's victims.

Hades is not to be confused with Hell. Hades is the temporary place for deceased unbelievers, until the final judgment. Hades will give up its dead at the final judgment, after which Hades (death) itself will join its occupants in Hell (see Revelation 20:14–15).

Read also Luke 21:11, 25.

The Fifth Seal

When the fifth seal was peeled back, it revealed a completely different scene from those of the four horsemen. Now John sees under the altar in heaven the souls of them that had been slain "for the word of God and the testimony which they held." Perhaps these are the martyrs Jesus referred to in Matthew 24:9.

In ancient sacrifices, the blood, which symbolized life, was poured out at the base of the altar. John saw the souls of all the Christian martyrs up until the time of the writing of Revelation, and by implication, until the Second Coming of Christ. They were praying for the vindication of God's justice, not for vengeance.

These martyrs are told to "rest a little while longer." God patiently delays the final judgment to give evildoers the opportunity to repent, even though His saints continue to suffer. God is concerned for justice, but even more for mercy.

The Sixth Seal

The terrible cosmic catastrophes which are predicted to occur in connection with the breaking of the sixth seal are almost inconceivable. The language is typically apocalyptic and symbolic. Yet, these events were predicted elsewhere as the beginning of the wrath of God. Compare the sixth seal with the predictions of Isaiah 34:4; Joel 2:30, 31 and Matthew 24:29.

Revelation 6:12 is kind of a pivot point in the otherwise age-long repetition of tribulation which Jesus predicted will occur when God expels evil from the earth. Men are finally going to see the seriousness of their circumstances, yet be unrepentant (Revelation 6:16).

Probing the Depths

There are three basic streams of judgment issuing from the throne, summarized in the sets of seven seals, seven trumpets, and seven vials (bowls). These judgments are not necessarily successive in occurrence, but seem to overlap, interweave, and finally culminate together. (Note that each set, in culminating, involves a great earthquake [Revelation 6:12; 11:13; 16:18], suggesting they deal with different time spans and/or arenas of divine judgment, but that they climax simultaneously.)

Kingdom Extra

Although the term "The Rapture" is not in the Bible, the idea it represents is clearly present. By "The Rapture" we refer to the literal, imminent (any moment) appearing of Jesus Christ from heaven, to take His redeemed church—the 'translated' living and the resurrected dead—to be with Him.

Since God has not appointed His church to wrath (1 Thessalonians 5:19), what does the fact that "His wrath has come" in Revelation 6:17 suggest about the timing of the promised deliverance?

The Sealing of the 144,000

It seems that times of tribulation give opportunity and motivation for witnessing. In Revelation 7, during an interlude in the dramatic descriptions of prophetic events, John sees two groups of people who will be especially used by God in grace during this period.

First are the 144,000 who will be "sealed" by God and protected from His wrath which is to come on the earth as judgment. Compare and contrast this "sealing" with those who will bear "the mark of the beast" in Revelation 13.

Probing the Depths

Three different views exist as to who the 144,000 may be.

The first is that they are a select group of Jewish converts to the Messiah who, in the wake of 'Tribulation' judgments (seven-year concept), turn to Jesus as Lord. They are then 'sealed' to preach the gospel to the world during this period after the church has been raptured.

The second is that they are a symbolic representation of the whole Church, including Jews and Gentiles (Romans 2:28, 29); a preserved people kept throughout the age long era of the tribulation (classical concept) as witnesses to Christ.

The third is that they represent the full measure of God's fulfilling His commitment to His chosen people, the Jews. The Word of God clearly states that He has not left Israel derelict from His purposes (Romans 9—11). Though they were "broken off" (Romans 11:17), there shall come a "resurrection" of His purposed will for national Israel (Romans 11:18) and a full complement of Jews shall be among the redeemed of all nations (Romans 11:26).

The Tribulation Believers

A second group of people to be uniquely used by God will be a mixed multitude of Gentiles. This great group is international in scope composed of many ethnic and geographic groups who are either saved during these difficult days, or, if they may represent the larger group of redeemed saints, throughout all history.

In Revelation 7:11, 12, God is worshipped by an especially lovely list of terms. Write below the seven elements of adoration which are ascribed to God "forever and ever. Amen."

 1. _____

2. _____

3. _____

4. _____

5. _____

6. _____

7. _____

This great multitude—which suddenly appears in heaven with white robes and palm branches—are so many that no one can number them. John has to ask who they are and where they came from (Revelation 7:13).

Many would understand the elder's response to indicate that this great multitude represents the true church which has been raptured and caught up to the throne of heaven before the great Day of the Lord (God's wrath) begins.

Kingdom Extra

Read Revelation 7.

In attempting to understand this verse, it is necessary to understand that *the ones who come out of* literally means "ones coming out," a present participle, expressing a continuous and repeated action, not a once-for-all action. The action suggests harmonies with the general tribulation that takes place throughout the entire church age. The Great Tribulation, however, describes the acceleration and intensification of troublesome times as the Age comes to an end, climaxing with the Rapture and Second Coming.

Read Matthew 13:21; John 16:33; Acts 14:22; Romans 8:35.

Questions:

To whom do these verses refer?

✎ _____

_____

_____

_____

_____

What does this mean in your own life?

✎ _____

_____

_____

_____

_____

The Seventh Seal

After the long interlude of Revelation 7, the final seal is broken and all heaven waits in anticipation for the fulfillment of God's purpose. This seventh seal released a second series of judgments: the seven trumpet judgments, which deluge a doomed planet with destructive demonic activity. These events begin the Great Tribulation which concludes with Christ's return.

Kingdom Life—*The Power of Praise*

The judgments which finally expel all evil from the earth are directly related to the praise, the worship, and the prayers of God's people. There may be no mightier statement in all the Bible on the truth of 'Kingdom entry through worship' than what is revealed in this Book. It is *present praise* that gives room for His presence and power among His people; and as shown in Revelation, it is *age-long worship* which releases His ultimate entry and dominion—the Forever Kingdom of our Lord (Revelation 19:1–7).

Read Psalms 22:3; 30:4–5.

Question:

What other Scriptures can you locate that give insight into the power of praise?

✎_____

_____

_____

_____

_____

Record Your Thoughts

Questions:

How is your "praise-life"? Our study in Revelation has revealed that present praise and accumulated adoration releases God's kingdom purposes. Rate yourself on a scale of 1–10 as a "present praiser."

✎_____

_____

_____

_____

Reread Revelation 4 and 5 and then write a paragraph of praise to God for who He is.

✎_____

_____

_____

_____

Review Revelation 7:9–12. Which aspects of adoration seem unclear to you?

✎_____

_____

_____

_____

ADDITIONAL OBSERVATIONS

The Proclamation

Revelation 8:2—15:4

Kingdom Key—*The Victory Is Won*

Romans 16:20 "And the God of peace will crush satan under your feet shortly. The grace of our Lord Jesus Christ be with you. Amen."

In this section of Revelation we see the cataclysmic travail of the last days. However the children of the kingdom endure it with a constant statement of the overcoming power of the blood of the Lamb and their transforming faith in Christ. Their faith is unwavering, the result of an abiding relationship with Jesus. This is the heart of faith's confession, based in God's Word and the blood of the Lamb, whose victory has provided the eternal conquest of satan.

Declare your abiding faith in the accomplished work of the Cross, and constantly participate in Jesus' ultimate victory, overcoming satan by the power of the Cross and the steadfastness of your confession of faith.

Read 1 John 5:4–5; 1 Corinthians 15:57–58.

Questions:

In what ways can the victory of the Cross affect our daily lives?

living in the victory of the cross

How can our choices, habits and actions inhibit our experience of this daily victory?

What steps can you take to ensure that will cause this victory to become more real in your life?

✎ _____

_____

_____

_____

The Judgments

It would seem that the seventh seal actually contains the seven trumpet judgments which call the waiting world to repentance. They differ from what preceded or follows.

- The seals reveal the *comprehensive* judgments released by God;
- the trumpets reveal the *controlling* judgments, the extent of which are restricted by God; and
- the vials reveal the *climaxing* judgments, which are poured out rapidly by the wrath of God.

Worship and intercession appear to be the two spiritual forces which release the seven severe trumpet judgments (Revelation 8:1–5).

Question:

Explain how worship and intercession can be considered "spiritual forces."

The Seven Trumpets

Read Revelation 8:2—11:18.

Trumpets are a warning signal and summons to repentance (see Exodus 19:16, 19). The plagues released by the blowing of the trumpets are reminiscent of the plagues of Egypt. The first four affect the natural world, and the last three affect the unredeemed. It is difficult to know to what degree these calamities are to be interpreted symbolically and not literally. It is clear, however, that the events are actual and cataclysmic; they are repetitive throughout history rather than consecutive; again they will intensify as the Age closes.

Significant symbolic elements in this portion of Revelation are:

1. **The golden altar**—the altar of incense as in the temple (8:3).
2. **A great mountain burning with fire**—suggests a meteor (8:8, 9).
3. **A star fallen from heaven**—refers to an unidentified demonic being, possibly satan (9:1).
4. **The bottomless pit**—literally "the shaft of the abyss," is the reservoir of evil, which acts as a prison for demons. It is also where satan will be bound (9:1).
5. **Smoke**—is a symbol of deception (9:2).
6. **Locusts**—symbolize demonic beings (9:1).

Questions:

Using the insights above, what do you believe the seven trumpet judgments symbolize?

_____

_____

_____

_____

Can you locate other Scriptures where heavenly beings are described similarly to the angel John saw in 10:1?

_____

_____

_____

What do you believe is the symbolism of the rainbow, the face like the sun, and feet like pillars of fire?

_____

_____

_____

How do these elements relate to your relationship with the Lord?

_____

_____

_____

The Little Book

Read Revelation 10:1–11.

John is instructed to eat the little book given to him by the angel. This is symbolic of the Word of God, the gospel, which John and the two witnesses (Revelation chapter 11) are to proclaim. The message must saturate the personality of the proclaimer. The Word of God must be completely assimilated into our very beings. It will then go forth in power to bring God's grace, love, and mercy to those who accept; but it will bring inevitable judgment when rejected.

The content of the message John is instructed to "eat" is uncertain, but the effect on John is both bitter and sweet. The judgments are sweet because they bring a proper end to evil. On the other hand, they are also bitter because of the wrath of God which will fall on the unrepentant.

The Temple

Read Revelation 11:1–14.

John is instructed to measure the "temple of God." The rod he is to use symbolizes either preservation or destruction; the context here indicates preservation. The temple of God symbolizes the people of God, the body of Christ. The altar in verse 1 is the altar of incense, symbolizing the prayers of the saints.

Read John 4:23–24; 9:31.

Question:

Why do you believe the angel gave instruction to "measure the temple of God . . . and those who worship there? What is the measure of a worshipper?

_____

_____

_____

 Probing the Depths

Though the "two witnesses" are not identified as individuals, they are reminiscent of Moses and Elijah as well as of Enoch and Elijah. One of Moses' greatest miracles was turning water into blood, and one of Elijah's was shutting up the sky.

However, man dies only once, and Moses died and is still buried on Mount Nebo in Jordan. Enoch and Elijah are the only two men who were taken by the Lord directly without dying (see Malachi 4:5, 6 and Mark 9:11–13).

Speculation abounds as to the identities of these two witnesses. Some consider they are actually two "companies" of appointed witnesses of God who are empowered in a special way during this time. Still others have suggested that the opening two verses are clearly spiritual and symbolic, so these witnesses are to be understood as totally symbolic elements. Regardless, we can be sure these witnesses *are* symbolic of the witnessing church, proclaiming the gospel and accompanied by signs and wonders.

These two witnesses—whoever they may be—will be supernaturally protected and given special anointed words to speak and special powers over nature (Revelation 11:5, 6).

Questions:

What is the major purpose of these witnesses?

_____

_____

_____

In what ways does the description of the ministry of the two witnesses also describe the call on the body of Christ?

_____

_____

_____

Kingdom Extra

In Revelation 11:12, a voice from heaven speaks to the resurrected witnesses and calls them to "'Come up here.' And they ascended to heaven in a cloud." Some people claim this verse describes the Rapture (1 Thessalonians 4:16, 17) and is symbolic of all the Christians going up into heaven. If so, then the Rapture occurs;

- at the end of the second half of Daniel's Seventieth Week,
- at the end of the Great Tribulation, and
- after the persecution of the Antichrist.

Some who hold to this time period for the Rapture see a similarity with the "clouds" which receive the two witnesses and the "clouds" in which both living and dead believers will be caught up at the Lord's return (Matthew 24:29, 30; 1 Thessalonians 4:15–18).

We cannot be dogmatic as to when the Rapture of the church will occur, but we can be assured that it will!

The Seventh Trumpet

As the seventh angel sounds the seventh (and last) trumpet (Revelation 11:15–19), the final triumph of God and Christ is proclaimed in terms of the reign of King Jesus over the earth and all eternity. There is transference of power and authority to the rightful Owner and true King: "The kingdoms of this world have become the kingdoms of our Lord and of His Christ, and He shall reign forever and ever!" (Revelation 11:15).

The content of the seventh trumpet is the future judgments of the bowls. In spite of the fact that much heavy judgment and suffering must come, these verses anticipate the glory of the coming reign of Christ on Earth.

Read Isaiah 55:12–13; Romans 8:21; 1 Corinthians 15:51–54.

Questions:

Which other Scriptures can you locate that describe the reign of Christ?

✎ _____

_____

_____

What will typify the Kingdom of our Lord?

✎ _____

_____

_____

Kingdom Life—*We Share Christ's Victory*

Read Revelation 12:1–17.

In this series of visions, specific events are pictured symbolically, emphasizing timeless principles of spiritual warfare. We are thus enabled to see the spiritual reality and meaning of events in our historical experience, such as the birth of the Messiah, together with satan's continuous attempts to destroy Him before He completed His redemptive work, and His exaltation, followed by the resultant persecution of His church. Knowing that they share in His victory will enable His people to endure patiently any future afflictions.

Questions:

Who does the "woman" represent?

_____

_____

_____

According to this passage, what is the key to overcoming?

_____

_____

_____

The Seven Signs

Up until this point, most of the Book of Revelation has concerned God's glory and His judgments against unbelievers on earth. Now, in the interlude indicated in Revelation 10—15, the drama shifts to seven *signs* (miniature vignettes) symbolically portraying portions of the Tribulation, not necessarily in chronological order.

The first scene presents an allegory in which the woman symbolizes God's people, the faithful remnant of Old Covenant Israel through whom the Messiah came forth.

Further symbolism in this scene identifies the dragon as satan. The number seven is the number of completion; therefore the seven heads represent complete authority and intelligence. Ten is the number representing *earthly* completeness and the horns symbolize physical or political strength; thus the meaning of ten horns is an all-powerful, earthly political system. Seven diadems represent political authority.

Questions:

How do the seven diadems identify the dragon with the last of the Gentile rulers of Daniel's dreams (Daniel 7:7, 8 and Revelation 13:1–7)?

✏️ _____

_____

_____

Who might be represented by "a third of the stars of heaven" (Revelation 12:7; Matthew 25:41; Ephesians 6:12)?

✏️ _____

_____

_____

Satan Thrown Out of Heaven

Read Revelation 12:7–17.

The second vignette depicts the same spiritual conflict as shown above (Revelation 12:1–6), but now it is described from the heavenly realm. The familiar passage of 12:11 reminds us that the brethren overcame the enemy during this time of persecution by appropriating the victory of the finished work of the Cross ("the blood of the Lamb") and by the patient, public confession of their faith ("the word of their testimony"). They loved Jesus more than life itself ("they did not love their lives to the death")!

Read Matthew 10:37–39.

Questions:

What are your reactions to this passage in Matthew?

✏️ _____

_____

_____

How does your love for the Lord measure up?

The Beast from the Sea

Read Revelation 13:1–10.

This first half of chapter 13 describes a hideous beast coming out of the sea. This is the first of two beasts who will have great authority and power in the rest of Revelation. The first will have great political power and the second (13:11), significant religious support to influence the political aims of the first.

This first beast, which rises "up out of the sea," is usually understood as the Antichrist John mentions in his smaller epistle (1 John 2:18).

Read Ephesians 6:12–18.

Questions

The Antichrist symbolizes and personifies all that is evil. How does the description of him in Revelation change the way you read the Ephesians passage?

Kingdom Extra

The biblical idea of the Antichrist is variously shown to be:

- A general spirit: (1 John 2:18, 22; 4:3; 2 John 7; Revelation 13:1, 2)
- The world's system: (Daniel 2:24, 25; 7:23–27)
- A human being: (Daniel 7:25; 8:22–26; 11:36–45; 2 Thessalonians 2:1–12)

Probing the Depths

A study of related passages (e.g., Daniel 7:23–27; 8:22–26; 11:36–45; Ezekiel 38:2, 4, 8, 9; 2 Thessalonians 2:1–12; Revelation 13:3; 17:8–11) reveal to some students of eschatology that this final Antichrist is a man who will come back to life following a fatal wound to the head by a military weapon, and who will rule the final beast empire of satan. How would a seemingly miraculous recovery/resurrection from such a wound enhance the power and authority of this new world dictator and the dragon?

The period of the beast's authority is limited. Compare Revelation 13:5 with 11:2, 3 and 12:6, 14, along with Daniel 9:27 and 12:6, 7. The Jews used the lunar year (comprised of 30-day months) to measure time. Consequently, in the interpretation of biblical prophecies, the application of the lunar year is generally accepted as a "prophetic year." Revelation 13:5–8 states that the Antichrist is empowered to blaspheme God and to make war with the saints for how many months? How many days would that be?

Read also Daniel 7:25; Revelation 11:2, 3; 12:6; 13:5–8.

The Beast from the Earth

Read Revelation 13:11–19.

Just as the first beast came up out of the sea (possibly the churning political chaos of modern governments), now John sees another beast coming up out of the earth. This beast will be the Antichrist's spokesperson, the False Prophet. He will direct people to worship the Antichrist.

The false prophet initiates a plan to attempt to force people to worship the image of the beast (v. 15).

Questions:

What is the connection between economics and worship in this evil plan?

✎ _____

_____

_____

What ways can you see in today's technology that could enable such a plan?

✎ _____

_____

_____

Behind the Scenes

Since neither the Hebrew nor the Greek language possessed a separate numerical system, the letters of their alphabets carried numerical value. Hence, the symbolic **number of the beast** is the sum of the numerical values of the separate letters of his name. The monster may be the last of many pseudo-Messiahs (see Matthew 24:24; Mark 13:22) to arise in history who manifest the spirit of antichrist.

Read 1 John 2:18, 19, 22; 4:3; 2 John 7.

Question:

What things do you see and hear in the world today that seem to set the stage for the Antichrist?

✎_____

_____

_____

The 144,000

Read Revelation 14:1–5.

The 144,000 symbolize all the faithful saints, the redeemed of the Lord. In verse 3, the vision of persecution abruptly changes to one of the church in glory singing a "new song" of redemption, which only the redeemed can understand. They stand on Mount Zion which is a spiritual reality expressing the communion of the saints, not a geographical place. These faithful ones bear the Father's name, in contrast to the mark "of the beast."

Read Ephesians 5:19; Colossians 3:16.

Questions:

Do you often experience a "song in your heart," in praise to God?

✎_____

_____

_____

What do you understand this song to represent?

✎_____

_____

_____

The Proclamation of Three Angels

Read Revelation 14:6–13.

In this scene we see three angels with three messages. The first angel (Revelation 14:6, 7) presents a call to all "who dwell on the earth" to honor the Creator. This "messenger" was evangelizing in the midst of judgment. There is no mention of Jewish evangelists or Christian witnesses, yet the grace of God provides the preaching of "the everlasting gospel" which is the gospel of Christ.

The second angel then flies with a declaration of doom. It announces the collapse Babylon, the Old Testament city filled with idolatry, the occult, and immorality. These evil practices inevitably result in the drinking of the cup of God's wrath.

The third angel warns of eternal judgment on those who are Beast-marked or worshippers of the Beast. Those who worship the Antichrist will suffer eternal punishment. There can be no compromise in the spiritual conflict.

All of these messages underscore the importance of patient endurance by the saints, who must "keep the commandments of God and the faith of Jesus."

Question:

What ongoing fruitfulness is promised to the dead in Christ?

✎_____

_____

_____

The Harvest

Read Revelation 14:14–20.

The harvest is used in the Old Testament as a symbol for divine judgment (Hosea 6:11; Joel 3:13). Likewise, Jesus related the final judgment to the harvest of the earth (Matthew 13:30, 39).

Many identify this vision of a two-phased harvest as the final eschatological judgment. Some interpret the first phase as believers being "harvested" from the earth and into the Lord's presence. The second harvest is often suggested as the ultimate wrath of God which is to be poured out on the unbelieving earth-dwellers in the bowl/vial judgments which follow in Revelation 16. Others see this second judgment as a restating of the first, emphasizing the kind and extent of judgment.

Read Hosea 6:11; Joel 3:13; Matthew 13:30, 39.

Questions:

In what ways is the Lord's gathering of His own like the harvesting of crops?

_____

_____

Would you consider yourself "ripe" and ready for harvest? Why?

_____

_____

Kingdom Life—*A Heart of Praise*

Read Revelation 15:1–4.

Revelation 15 begins with a celestial interlude which serves as a prelude to the last series of seven punitive plagues (Revelation 15:1). The plagues are preceded by various victorious saints singing special songs of praise for the redemption which is theirs. They sing the song of Moses and the song of the Lamb.

Read Exodus 15:1–18.

Questions:

Why is the song of Moses appropriate at this time?

_____

_____

_____

Why do you believe the Lord showed John an interlude of praise just prior to the last of the judgments?

✎ _____

_____

_____

_____

What can we learn from this that will enable us to live our lives in the Lord more fearlessly and with greater strength?

✎ _____

_____

_____

_____

Record Your Thoughts

Questions:

Do you experience present victory in the Lord?

✎ _____

_____

What do you believe hinders you from this experience?

✎ _____

_____

_____

_____

What can you learn from this session that will translate into direction for everyday life?

✎ _____

_____

_____

_____

SESSION ELEVEN

The Testimony
Revelation 15:5—20:3

 Kingdom Key—*Show Forth His Glory*

2 Thessalonians 1:10–12 "... when He comes, in that Day, to be glorified in His saints and to be admired among all those who believe, because our testimony among you was believed. Therefore we also pray always for you that our God would count you worthy of *this* calling, and fulfill all the good pleasure of *His* goodness and the work of faith with power, that the name of our Lord Jesus Christ may be glorified in you, and you in Him, according to the grace of our God and the Lord Jesus Christ."

Jesus said he came to bring glory to the Father. The meaning of the word glory transcends any common use of today. This glory is the showing forth of the Spirit of God; making God known and revealing to the world the character of our Father.

Jesus glorified the Father, displaying on Earth the splendor of a wondrously real and loving God. When humankind saw Jesus, they saw the Father. Further, Jesus brought glory to the Father by completing the work the Father gave Him.

To glorify God then, is to complete an assignment—to do those things He has called, chosen, appointed, and anointed us to do.

Read John 17:4–26; Matthew 25:31; Colossians 1:9–15.

Questions:

With these Scriptures in mind, what is the primary call on the life of a believer?

✎ _____

_____

_____

We are to show forth the nature of our Father. When others look at you, what attributes would they assign to our Father?

✎ _____

_____

_____

The Seven Bowls

Read Revelation 15:5—16:21.

If the first phase of the final judgment (Revelation 14:14–16) represents believers being "harvested" from the earth and into the Lord's presence, then Revelation 15 can be thought of as a detailed account of what happens to them in heaven. Likewise, chapter 16 details what transpires in the second phase for those who have embraced evil on the earth.

While the seals and the trumpets picture partial judgments, the seven bowls picture judgments that are about to be consummated, and thus are the last.

Behind the Scenes

The "temple of the tabernacles of the testimony" which is opened in verse 5 is, literally, "the tent of witness." This is exactly the same word from the Greek text of Exodus 40:34, 35, describing the ancient tabernacle. The tabernacle was God's dwelling place on earth.

Read the description of the tabernacle in Exodus or locate a trusted Bible resource which describes the tabernacle and its furnishings. Note how the symbolic elements are repeated throughout the book of Revelation.

Word Wealth—*Testimony*

Testimony: Greek, *marturion* (mar-too'-ree-on); Strong's 3142: Compare the words "martyr" and "martyrdom." This word means proof, evidence, witness, or proclamation of personal experience. The tabernacle, which evidences God's presence, is a testimony to the covenant between Him and His people.

The Seven Bowl Angels

Read Revelation 15:6—16:1.

From the heavenly counterpart of the earthly "tabernacle of testimony," seven angels, dressed as priests and carrying seven plagues, came out to execute the wrath of God in the earth; to pour out His final judgment. (The number seven appears repeatedly throughout Scripture, especially the book of Revelation. It is the number symbolizing completion, so its meaning here is clear.)

The angels come out of the temple which is filled with "smoke from the glory of God." Once they leave, the temple and the mercy seat (the place of God's grace and forgiveness) are no longer accessible. No further petitions or intercessions will be heard until the Final Judgment is completed.

Read Exodus 40:34, 35; 1 Kings 8:10, 11; Isaiah 6:1–4.

Questions:

What other Scriptures can you find that speak of this "holy smoke?"

_____

_____

_____

What do you believe the symbolism behind this smoke may be?

_____

_____

_____

The Seven Plagues

Read Revelation 16:2–21.

While the seven bowls have certain similarities to the seven trumpets, there are pronounced differences. The plagues introduced by the trumpets were partial and constituted a call to repentance. The bowls are the execution of total judgment when there is no more hope of repentance.

The bowl judgments include:

1. Horrible sores on the Beast-marked, verse 2
2. Sea polluted into total devastation, verse 3 (8:8, 9)
3. Waters turn to blood—pollution, verses 4–7 (8:10, 11)
4. Sun scorches mankind, verses 8, 9.
5. Darkness and pain on the power brokers, verses 10, 11 (9:6)
6. The last surge of demonic furies, verses 12–16 (9:13–15)
7. The final shaking of the Earth, verses 17–21 (6:12–17; 11:15–19; Hebrews 12:25–29).

 Kingdom Life—*Watch and Pray*

Read Revelation 16:15.

How is this Scripture both a hope-filled promise for the believer and a haunting prediction for the unbeliever?

Read Luke 12:39, 40; 2 Peter 3:10; Revelation 3:3; Matthew 24:45–47.

Questions:

What do these passages teach us about believers and end times?

_____

_____

_____

How do we serve the Lord in the meantime?

_____

_____

_____

In light of these Scriptures, are you ready?

_____

_____

_____

Armageddon

Read Revelation 16:12–16.

The frogs in the sixth plague emerge from the unholy, counterfeit trinity: the dragon, the beast (Antichrist) and the false prophet. These frogs symbolize their demonic work.

However, though totally unaware of it, these three beings are used by god to accomplish His purpose, to gather the kings of the earth to the last great battle.

The location of this gathering is Armageddon, which may refer to the Mount of Megiddo, Israel's chief battlefield in ancient time. It may be that this is not a literal military conflict as no battle is described. In any case, it is a spiritually decisive conflict involving the final over-throw of the enemy by the power of Almighty God.

 Probing the Depths

Read Revelation 16:17–21.

The seventh bowl differs in that it is not poured out on the earth, but rather "into the air." We are not told what this means. Some see significance in that this is said to be the abode of satan, the "prince of the powers of the air" (Ephesians 2:2). Others feel it indicates that this last judgment is universal.

Once the seventh bowl is emptied, the "voice" from the "temple of heaven" declares that the plagues are complete and the end has arrived. This is followed by severe, cataclysmic earthquakes and hail. Each hailstone is reported to weigh "a talent" which is equivalent to 57–79 pounds! Just as the law of Israel required the stoning to death of the blasphemers and adulterers, so here the blasphemers and adulterers, fornicators and harlots (idolaters) of the end time shall be stoned to death from Heaven!

The Demonic and The Divine

Read Revelation 17:1–18.

Just as the unrepentant people of earth were judged because of their wickedness, the major perpetrators of evil will likewise meet their just rewards in God's prophetic timetable. With graphic detail, John relates dramatic displays of the demonic and Divine as God judges the Antichrist, False Prophet, and satan, and the systems they controlled.

John draws our attention to one city in particular, referring to it as "the great harlot." A harlot is a woman who fornicates for financial or commercial gain, and the city is Babylon, symbolic of every type of idolatrous system opposed to Christ. Just as Roman prostitutes were required to wear a label with their names on their foreheads, Babylon bore the mark of her idolatry.

In Revelation 17:7–11 the angel acknowledges to John the meanings behind the mystery of some of these symbols. He focuses on the beast which has seven heads and ten horns. This final beast empire represents all the previous seven beast empires, five of which had come and gone ("five have fallen"), "one is," and one was still to come in the future and would "continue for a short time."

The ten horns in Revelation 17:12, 13 are said to represent the ten-nation federation which will give its power and strength to the beast (compare Daniel 7:23, 24 with Revelation 13:1). United, they will gather to make war with the Lamb, seeking to prevent Him from setting up His universal messianic kingdom (Revelation 19:19). Armageddon decides their awful fate.

The scarlet woman is both a religious system and a city (Revelation 17:18) which will "ride the beast" for a while. But finally, when the worship of the Beast is set in place (Revelation 13:4, 14, 15), the coalition of kings will resist her chokehold on their freedom and finances and react with vengeance. She will be destroyed by the very beast (forces of Antichrist) upon which she rode to influence and power.

Read Ezekiel 38:2, 14–17; Daniel 11:36; Matthew 24:15–21; 2 Thessalonians 2:2–4, 9; Revelation 12:13–7; 13:3, 12; 17:8.

Question:

It is important that we be informed as to the character and signs of the Antichrist. What do these Scriptures tell us about him?

✎ _____

_____

_____

The Fall of Babylon

Read Revelation 18:1–24.

Seven voices describe the fall of Babylon as an accomplished fact, some in thanksgiving and others in dismay. Babylon in the New Testament is a symbol of sinful humanity and its capacity for self-delusion, ambition, sinful pride, and demonized depravity. It represents world culture in rebellion against God. Babylon stands in contrast to the church as a society that persecutes God's people and will inevitably be destroyed.

Behind the Scenes

When the Book of Revelation was written, Babylon may have been a kind of code name for pre-Christian Rome that was built on seven hills (Revelation 17:9) and which was already persecuting the church. Since that time, generations of Christians have been able to identify their own Babylons and have found reassurance in Revelation's message.

Kingdom Life—*Shout "Alleluia!"*

Read Revelation 19:1–10.

A great multitude in heaven (the "Church Triumphant") begins to rejoice over the fall of Babylon. Twice in this spontaneous expression of praise the word "Alleluia" is used. This word (which means "praise the Lord") occurs in the New Testament only in this particular passage of praise. In Revelation 19:5 a voice comes from the throne admonishing the saints to praise the Lord. Then the great multitude responds and rejoices!

Read Psalm 22:3.

Question:

With this Scripture in mind, why is praise most logical and most important at this time?

_____

_____

_____

Kingdom Extra

Read Revelation 19:6–10.

The Lord illustrates the restoration of His intimacy with His people through the analogy of the bride and Bridegroom. This passage depicts the wedding feast of the Lamb, Jesus, when He claims His bride, the church, after she has made herself ready for Him. The bride will prepare herself by submitting to God and allowing herself to be cleansed by the washing of His Word, so that she may be presented to the Bridegroom without spot, wrinkle, or blemish.

When the bride is prepared and Jesus returns for her, the intimacy broken in the Garden will be completely restored, and man will again become one with Christ and with God. But, as in the first "marriage" between Adam and Eve, the bride must be bone of His bones and flesh of His flesh—that is, she must be like Him. He will not return for a defiled, defeated bride. In these days of restoration, God is preparing the bride with beauty and power and dressing her in His glory.

Read Matthew 22:11–14; Ephesians 5:25–27; John 17:20–26.

Questions:

What analogies exist within the relationship of marriage that portray the relationship between Christ and His church?

✎_____

_____

_____

_____

With this in mind, what is lacking in your relationship with the Lord that weakens your bond with Him?

✎_____

_____

_____

_____

Kingdom Life—*Behold, He Comes!*

Read Revelation 19:11–21.

The exciting Second Coming of Jesus Christ to Earth is recorded in the remainder of Revelation 19. The returning Savior's characteristics, companions, and conquests are given as the culmination toward which all of the Book of Revelation has been moving.

Jesus originally entered Jerusalem as the Messiah riding on a lowly donkey (Zechariah 9:9; Matthew 21:1–11). This time He comes on a white horse, the symbol of conquest and victory! Jesus comes to execute judgment in the court of the law, not on the battlefield. He conducts a spiritual warfare, not a military one.

His impending victory is celebrated with the "marriage supper of the Lamb." And is followed by a "supper of the great God," which is a grisly feast as birds of prey devour the idolatrous unredeemed. This is a solemn contrast to the celebratory feast of the redeemed with their Bridegroom and Lord.

The Antichrist and false prophet will meet their end in the lake of fire and their allies will be slain by the Word of the Lord, which has power to overcome all evil.

Probing the Depths

Read Revelation 20:1–3.

There are basically two broad positions regarding the reign of Christ during the 1,000-year period, or Millennium, referred to in Revelation 20. The *premillennial view* holds that after the victory in Revelation 19, Christ will set up an earthly kingdom and will reign with the resurrected saints in peace and righteousness for 1,000 years, which may be a literal period or may be symbolic of an undetermined period. At the end of this period satan will lead a final rebellion which will fail, and the world to come begins.

The *realized millennial view* (also called amillennial or present millennial) holds that the 1,000 years symbolize the period between the two advents of Christ, either as fully or progressively being realized. In this view, the millennial kingdom is a spiritual, not a political, reign of saints, being realized with Christ now, whether the believer is in heaven or on Earth.

Whatever one's interpretation of the Millennium, the central truth of the defeat of satan in stages remains the same.

Kingdom Life—*The Kingdom Within*

While it is stimulating to study about the future reign of Christ with His saints here on earth, it is important to remember that He is **today** King of kings and Lord of lords.

Jesus taught his disciples that the "kingdom of God is within you" (Luke 17:21). As we walk with Him in obedience and holiness, His authority and anointing is transferred to us to transact His kingdom's business in His stead. The full consummation of His kingdom awaits His literal, physical return. Until that time, let us serve Him using the "keys of the kingdom" He has granted us.

Read Isaiah 61:1–3; Luke 4:18; John 1:16; 1 John 2:20, 27; 4:17.

Questions:

What should characterize Christ's ambassadors?

_____

_____

_____

Does your life show forth the kingdom to others?

_____

_____

_____

What steps can you take to increase your effectiveness in the kingdom?

_____

_____

_____

Record Your Thoughts

Questions:

Why is a lifestyle of praise important?

✎ _____

_____

_____

_____

_____

How should we respond to the trials of today, recognizing Christ's ultimate victory?

✎ _____

_____

_____

_____

_____

What has impacted you most in this session?

✎ _____

_____

_____

_____

_____

What effect will this have on your everyday life?

✎ _____

_____

_____

_____

ADDITIONAL OBSERVATIONS

SESSION TWELVE

The Reward

Revelation 20:4—22:21

 Kingdom Key—*Hold Fast to the Faith*

Galatians 6:8–9 "For he who sows to his flesh will of the flesh reap corruption, but he who sows to the Spirit will of the Spirit reap everlasting life. And let us not grow weary while doing good, for in due season we shall reap if we do not lose heart."

God has a timetable for every seed. His timetable is not ours; sometimes "due season" comes quickly and sometimes we must wait. But we can count on three things: God will cause a harvest to come, God is never early or late, the harvest will bear the same nature as the seeds that are sown.

Regardless, know that a harvest is guaranteed and the final harvest will come. Continue to hold fast to the faith, planting righteous seeds. And watch for your reward with an attitude of expectancy.

Read Hebrews 11:6; Luke 6:20–36.

Questions:

According to the Beatitudes, what seeds lead to reward?

✎ _____

_____

_____

Describe this reward.

✎ _____

_____

_____

The Reign of Christ

Read Revelation 20:4–6.

The 1,000-year millennial period sits like a peaceful valley between the last two great battles of the world: the campaign of Armageddon (Revelation 19:11–21) and the rebellion of Gog and Magog (Revelation 20:7–10). In this long-awaited setting the King consummates His rule and reign on earth.

It is at this point that the first resurrection takes place. These resurrected ones are: many dead saints of Old Testament times (see Matthew 27:52, 53), the dead saints of the church, those martyred for their testimony during the Great Tribulation, and those who are taken up in the rapture.

They are the priests of God and of Christ. It is the ministry of the priesthood to continually serve and minister to the Lord. The life of a priest is consecrated wholly to the Lord. It is through this consecrated, surrendered heart that we will be enabled to reign with Him.

Read Revelation 1:6; 5:10.

Questions:

What are the duties of a priest?

✎ _____

_____

_____

What are the duties of a king?

✎ _____

_____

_____

With that in mind, what is the call on our lives as kings and priests of God?

✎ _____

_____

_____

Kingdom Life—*Satan Is a Defeated Foe*

Read Revelation 20:7–10.

Over all the ages, it has been satan's purpose and desire to so frustrate God's purpose and in that way, to limit the scope of His salvation. This last attempted battle is no exception. All the rulers and their peoples who ally with satan in this final rebellion surround the residence of the resurrected saints. However, no military battle takes place as the enemy cannot withstand the overwhelming power of God. Although satan was condemned at the Cross, his final sentencing was stayed until our sovereign God was through using him for His own purposes. Satan suffers final and utter defeat as he is cast into the lake of fire prepared for him and his angels.

History has ended. Only the Final Judgment remains to complete the drama of redemption.

Read Psalms 78:68; 87:2.

Questions:

What do we know about God's love for Jerusalem?

_____

_____

How does this affect us today?

_____

_____

_____

What does it mean that you are one of God's beloved?

_____

_____

How does this affect your life and choices?

_____

_____

_____

Probing the Depths

At the end of the 1,000 years, *satan will be released* in the Earth again *to deceive*. It appears that many who submitted to Christ's rule during the Millennium did so without inner commitment to His lordship. The final deception of satan separates these from those who have sincerely submitted. This is the last insurrection that the Lord will tolerate. Satan will next be *cast into the lake of fire and tormented . . . forever.*

The Great White Throne of Judgement

Read Revelation 20:11–15.

We are all going to stand before the King of kings some day. He is going to judge all men; whether saved or lost, they are going to appear before Him. The believers will appear before Him at the judgment which we call the Bema seat of Christ to see whether they receive a reward (see 2 Corinthians 5:10). The lost will come before Him at the Great White Throne. Remember that the Lord Jesus did not come to judge the first time, but He will come as Judge the next time, and *all* judgment is committed to Him. All who have rejected Him will be found guilty and every believer will stand before Him to see whether or not he will receive a reward.

Read Matthew 12:36, 37; Romans 2:5–10.

Questions:

How do you feel that all your actions and words will be judged by our Lord?

✎ _____

_____

_____

What steps can you take that will enable you to make better choices in the future?

✎ _____

_____

_____

What Scriptures can you locate that will assist you in your efforts?

_____

_____

_____

A New Heaven and a New Earth

Read Revelation 21:1–8.

God originally created the earth and the heavenly atmosphere which surrounds it to be man's permanent home. He declared it "good" and delegated His rule over planet earth to man. But when man fell from his place of relationship with God, he also forfeited his right to rule this earth.

Since that time "the whole creation groans and labors with birth pangs . . . until now" (Romans 8:22) as satan's destructive designs were multiplied. In Revelation 21, with satan removed, God's redemption reaches even to His creation as He renovates both heaven and earth.

Not only has God planned a *new environment* for his people, but also a *new experience of intimacy.*

Read 1 Corinthians 13:12; Revelation 21:3.

Questions:

What does Paul mean by "we see in a mirror, dimly?"

_____

_____

_____

What is "that which is perfect?"

_____

_____

_____

What does it mean that God has chosen to "tabernacle" within us?

_____

_____

_____

The New Jerusalem

Read Revelation 21:9—22:5.

If the New Jerusalem is the bride of Christ, and if Christians are the inhabitants of that city, then this passage is referring to the believers—the inhabitants of the New Jerusalem—as the bride of Christ.

This New Jerusalem, the capital city of the "new heaven and new earth," and is built in a perfect cube, a very clear symbol of perfection. It is perfect in its universality and its holiness. It is also unique for what is not there.

Read Revelation 21:4, 22–23, 25, 27; 22:3, 5; 21:25, 27.

Question:

What will be missing in The New Jerusalem?

✎ _____

_____

_____

Even So, Come, Lord Jesus

Read Revelation 22:6–21.

However long our current era of the Spirit continues, the next act in God's universal drama is the consummation of the ages. Seven witnesses testify to the authenticity of this message: God (through His angel), John, the witness of the angel, the Lord Jesus, the Spirit, the bride and him who hears. The climactic focus of the Revelation is an evangelistic appeal addressed to those who still remain outside, "Come!"

 Kingdom Life—*He will Return*

Among the very last words of the Bible is this promise from the Lord Jesus, 'Surely I am coming quickly.' This blessed hope, which was declared by angels and spoken of by the apostles, is tenderly reiterated by the Lord at the very end of His Word. It is as if He wished to say, 'There is much in My Word that you need attend to, but do not let this hope be overshadowed: I am coming back soon.' Together with John, let us say, 'Even so, come, Lord Jesus!'

Record Your Thoughts

Questions:

What do you believe Jesus means when He says, "I am the Alpha and Omega?"

_____

_____

_____

Give any insight you might have into the words "Bright and Morning Star."

_____

_____

_____

What feelings do you now experience when you contemplate the imminent return of our Lord?

_____

_____

_____

How will keeping the words of Revelation in mind help you walk more faithfully with the Lord?

_____

_____

_____

Conclusion

Jesus calls His people to be fully separated from the word's value system and to be totally committed to Him. Christ is to be the spiritual power source of our lives. We should gauge our success by the measuring rod of God, not the world's social and financial standard. When we understand God's view from the eternal, the present comes into correct perspective.

Through the words of Daniel and Revelation, we are allowed a glimpse at our world and history through the eyes of their Creator. We can learn much about how to walk today by realizing and internalizing God's perspective.

Probing the Depths

Review the Kingdom Keys as they have been presented in this study of Daniel and Revelation and, after each, write the insights you have gained in this study. Allow the Spirit of God to quicken in your spirit the powerful messages these books contain for your life today.

1. **Hear the Word of God**

_____

_____

_____

_____

2. **Hold to the Promise**

_____

_____

_____

_____

3. **Prepare Your Heart**

_____

_____

_____

_____

4. **Listen and Yield**

_____

_____

_____

5. Seek Understanding

_____
_____
_____

6. Pray Without Ceasing

_____
_____
_____

7. Take Your Stand

_____
_____
_____

8. Be a Partaker of Life

_____
_____
_____

9. Press into Worship

_____
_____
_____

10. Trust in God

_____
_____
_____

11. Show Forth His Glory

✎ _____

_____

_____

_____

12. Hold Fast to Faith

✎ _____

_____

_____

_____

The wise believer takes the time to hear what the Spirit is saying to the church. This is as needed today as it was in the first century. If you hear and follow the voice of the Holy Spirit you do not need to fear the tactics of the enemy. Rather, you will be enabled to walk victoriously where Jesus requires and grow in the things of the Spirit of God. You will be enabled to enter in to the spiritual victory Christ has already won. And you will one day hear the most precious words of all, "Well done, good and faithful servant. Enter in . . ."